THE **FORTEAN TIMES** BOOK OF

Strange Deaths

THE **FORTEAN TIMES** BOOK OF
STRANGE DEATHS

COMPILED BY
Paul Sieveking

DESIGN & ILLUSTRATIONS
Etienne Gilfillan

EDITOR -IN-CHIEF
David Sutton

PUBLISHING & MARKETING
Russell Blackman
020 7907 6488
russell_blackman@dennis.co.uk

BOOKAZINE MANAGER
Dharmesh Mistry
020 7907 6100
dharmesh_mistry@dennis.co.uk

THE FORTEAN TIMES BOOK OF STRANGE DEATHS is
published by Dennis Publishing Ltd, 30 Cleveland Street,
London W1T 4JD. Company registered in England. The
MagBook brand is a trademark of Dennis Publishing Ltd.
All material © Dennis Publishing Ltd, licensed by Felden
2011, and may not be reproduced in any form without
the consent of the publishers.
The Fortean Times Book of Strange Deaths
ISBN 1-907779-97-3

All material copyright 2011.
Printed at Stones Printers Limited.

LICENSING AND SYNDICATION
To license this product, contact Hannah Heagney:
020 7907 6134 / hannah_heagney@dennis.co.uk
For syndication enquiries, contact Anj Dosaj-Halai:
020 7907 6132 /anj_dosaj-halai@dennis.co.uk

LIABILITY
While every care was taken during the production of this
MagBook, the publishers cannot be held responsible for
the accuracy of the information or any consequence
arising from it. Dennis Publishing takes no responsibility
for the companies advertising in this MagBook. The
paper used within this MagBook is produced from
sustainable fibre, manufactured by mills with a valid
chain of custody.

DENNIS PUBLISHING LTD
Digital Production Manager: Nicky Baker
Operations Director: Robin Ryan
MD of Advertising: Julian Lloyd-Evans
Newstrade Director: David Barker
Publisher: Russell Blackman
Chief Operating Officer: Brett Reynolds
Group Finance Director: Ian Leggett

Chief Executive: James Tye
Chairman: Felix Dennis

HOW TO CONTACT US
MAIL: 30 Cleveland Street, London W1T 4JD
PHONE: 020 7907 6000
EMAIL AND WEB
Website: www.forteantimes.com

To contact advertising:
Ciaran Scarry 020 7907 6683
ciaran_scarry@dennis.co.uk

CONTENTS

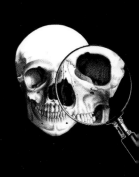

CHAPTER 1

Oops!

Accidents will happen, and many of them - involving
everything from electricity to flying lamb chops and
homemade sex toys - inevitably prove fatal...

A DWARF NICKNAMED OD DIED in a circus accident in northern Thailand. According to the *Pattaya Mail*, he "bounced sideways from a trampoline and was swallowed by a yawning hippopotamus which was waiting to appear in the next act. Vets on the scene said Hilda the Hippo had a gag reflex that automatically caused her to swallow." The vets said it was the first time the hefty vegetarian had ever eaten a circus performer. "Unfortunately, the 1,000-plus spectators continued to applaud wildly until commonsense dictated that there had been a tragic mistake." *Melbourne Herald Sun, 16 July 1999.*

MICHAEL COLOMBINI, SIX, WAS undergoing tests in a magnetic resonance imaging machine in Westchester Medical Center, Valhalla, New York State, on 27 July 2001 to determine his progress after surgery for a benign brain tumour when the machine's 10-ton electromagnet slammed a metal oxygen tank against him, crushing his skull. He died two days later. The tank was moved to the room accidentally after the boy was already in the machine. The magnet is about 30,000 times as powerful as Earth's magnetic field, and 200 times stronger than a common refrigerator magnet. In 2000, an MRI magnet in Rochester, New York, pulled a .45-calibre gun out of a police officer's hand and discharged a shot. No one was hurt. *[AP] 31 July 2001.*

A 28-YEAR-OLD IRANIAN BRIDEGROOM died instantly when he licked honey from his bride's finger during their marriage ceremony in the northwestern city of Qazvin and choked to death on one of her false nails. The bride was rushed to hospital after fainting from shock. Iranian couples lick honey from each other's fingers when they get married so that their life together starts sweetly. *[R] 12 Dec 2001.*

GEORGE KAFATOS, A CUSTOMER IN A crowded Athens restaurant, was killed by a flying lamb chop when an oven exploded. Five other diners were hurt. *Sunday Mercury, 10 June 2001.*

TWO HAPLESS CHINESE THIEVES GASSED themselves to death with cyanide along with five intended victims while trying to rob a gambling den in the city of Ruichang in June 2005. In May 2006, a court in nearby Jiujiang sentenced their three surviving accomplices to death. One of the three passed out for several hours from the effects of the gas – but still remembered to rob the dead of 15,950 yuan, five mobile phones and a gold necklace when he came around. *[R] 1 May 2006.*

MARIESA WEBER, 38, RETURNED TO HER family home in New Port Richey, Florida, on 28 October 2006 and greeted her mother, after which she wasn't seen again. Her family thought she had been kidnapped and contacted the authorities. Relatives scoured her room for clues but found nothing, although they did notice a strange smell, which they blamed on rats. Almost two weeks later, on 9 November, Mariesa's sister Gia went into her bedroom and saw a foot protruding from behind a bookcase. Using a torch, the family saw Mariesa was wedged upside-down behind the bookcase. It is believed she fell over as she tried to adjust a television plug behind the 6ft (1.8m) unit. The sheriff's office said Mariesa, who was only 5ft 3in (1.6m) and weighed barely 100lb (45kg), appeared to have died because she was unable to breathe in the position she was in. Both Mariesa and Gia previously had adjusted the television plug by standing on a bureau next to the bookcase and leaning over the top. *[AP] 25 Nov; D.Mail, 27 Nov 2006.*

JAMES 'LOCKY' BYRNE, 84, WAS KILLED instantly when he was hit by a flying horseshoe as he drove along a country lane outside Callan, Co. Kilkenny, Ireland, at 5.30pm on 16 May 2007. A local farmer had stretched a white tape across the lane to stop the cattle he was herding from wandering off. One end of the tape had been attached to a horseshoe, which was then secured to the branch of an overhanging tree. Mr Byrne, of Cottertown in Callan, was unaware of the obstruction in his path. The fabric stretched as it came into contact with the front grille of his old Datsun. Because of the pressure, the horseshoe freed itself from the bent branch, flew towards the car, smashed through the side window and hit Mr Byrne on the temple. *D.Mail, Irish Examiner, 14 June 2007.*

ENERGY KAMURUKO, 20, WAS OUT TRACKING with dogs in Zimbabwe on 10 October 2010 when he noticed a rabbit dart into a tunnel near the village of Mandipaka. He peered inside but his head got stuck. A neighbour found his body the following day and a post mortem confirmed he died of asphyxiation. It was the second hunting-related accidental death in Zimbabwe in recent months. In August, Tamsen Lucius, 36, impaled himself on his own spear while chasing wild boar. He had climbed a tree to get a better spear-throwing angle, but lost his footing and impaled himself through the chest. *Metro, 15 Oct 2010.*

IN 1988, GERALD JACKSON, 53, RETURNED drunk to his home in Newton Aycliffe, Durham, and used a key on a string around his neck to unlock his front door. He tripped when the wind blew open the door, and he was strangled.

On 7 April 1999, Beatrice Thornton, 73, fell while trying to open the door of her fifth-floor apartment in Pittsburgh with a key that was around her neck, strangling herself. The key remained in the door lock and her body weight held the strap tightly around her neck.

In February 2003, Kieran Duggal, 53, leant forward to unlock his front door with a key tied round his neck. He slipped and became tangled, accidentally throttling himself. Jobless Mr Duggal was found dead outside his home in Balham, southwest London. The Consumer Product Safety Commission has no reference in its files to adult deaths from key straps. *Victoria (BC) Times-Colonist, 11 June 1988; [AP] 9 April 1999; D.Express, 19 Feb 2003.*

〜 SUZANNE CORNWALL, 18, DIED AFTER HER scarf got caught in a go-kart engine and strangled her at Cambridgeshire Raceway at an after-hours session with friends on 10 December 2009. A track marshal who allowed the teenagers to race without the normal security precautions was sacked and faced prosecution. The same fate befell a Muslim woman, who was strangled to death in Sydney, Australia, when her hijab tangled up in the wheels of a go-kart on 9 April 2010. The 24-year-old's headscarf wrapped around a wheel axle as she raced and quickly tightened around her neck. She went into cardiac arrest and was airlifted to hospital, but died soon after. The deaths echoed that of dancer Isadora Duncan, whose scarf caught in the open-spoked wheel of a car in Nice in 1927. *Metro, 15 Dec 2009; (Sydney) D.Telegraph, 9 April 2010.*

〜 DOCTOR MICHELLE FERRARI-GEGERSON, 37, died when her electric neck massage machine caught on her necklace and strangled her in Fort Lauderdale, Florida, on Christmas Eve 2010. *Sun, 30 Dec 2010.*

WHEN GIL SARENTIS, 52, OF TAMPA, Florida, accidentally flushed $40 down his lavatory, he refused to give up the cash as lost. Instead, he opened his 1,000-gallon septic tank, was overcome by the methane fumes, fell in face first, and drowned. *News of the World, 30 Aug; Guardian, 5 Sept 1998.*

THOMAS WOODS AND ROD BENNETT WERE at the former's Long Island home getting seriously sozzled. Then Woods had an idea to liven things up. He set fire to the rug and challenged his friend to see who could stay in the house the longest. The late Mr Woods won. *Independent on Sunday, 25 April 2004.*

RADICAL RIBEIRO, THE DIRECTOR OF AN Angolan crime film, said police shot dead two of his actors after mistaking them for real armed robbers. They were carrying unloaded firearms as they filmed a scene in a rough suburb of the capital, Luanda, in December 2007. Ribeiro said he had permission to film in the area. The police arrived in a pickup truck and "started shooting at everybody at close range," he said. "They went on shooting until I shouted out: 'Please don't shoot, this is a movie!'" The officers then stopped firing and left without attending to the wounded, who were taken to hospital. *BBC News, 18 Dec 2007.*

A 43-YEAR-OLD UKRAINIAN man was electrocuted when he used a live electric cable connected to the mains in his house to kill fish in the river Tereblya. When the dead fish appeared on the water surface, he went to collect his take before turning off the power. According to the *Fakty* newspaper, he had intended to cook the fish for a meal to mark the first anniversary of his mother-in-law's death. *[DPA] 27 May 1999.*

SALIAMIN AKRAMI, 32, AN AFGHAN asylum-seeker residing in Willesden, west London, accidentally killed himself on 23 October 1999 by urinating on a live rail at the deserted Kensal Green railway station. Six hundred volts formed an arc into the tip of his penis, causing him to convulse and collapse on the rail. The alcohol in his blood was more than twice the drink-drive limit, and it was likely he was drunk. Pathologist Rufus Crompton identified the cause of death by a tiny, precise burn mark to the urinary opening of the penis. *Guardian, 10 Mar 2000.*

THE SAME FATE BEFELL A POLISH tourist at Vauxhall station in south London on 12 July 2008. The 41-year-old married teacher died after he crept into a recess for a pee. It is thought the urine splashed on the line, which carried 750 volts. About 40 per cent of Britain's 10,200 miles (16,500km) of train track is electrified. Staff found his body after he was filmed on CCTV going into the nook and failing to come out again. It was believed he was on a visit to Britain to improve his English. *Sun, 22 July 2008.*

THE TRADITIONAL PRE-CHRISTMAS SWINE slaughter in the Hungarian village of Darvaspuszta turned to tragedy on 24 November 2001 when an unnamed Croat was electrocuted attempting to knock out a pig with a homemade pig-stunner.

Then a local man was hospitalised with an irregular heart rhythm after attempting a rescue by trying to unplug the device. The pig's owner was so shocked by all this that he suffered a fatal heart attack. There was no word on the fate of the pig. *[R] Observer, 25 Nov 2001.*

A 47-YEAR-OLD WOMAN IN THE SPANISH town of Rivero de Posedas was strangled to death by her scarf after it got stuck in a tumble dryer on 11 December. She had put a load of washing in the machine and switched it on without realising the end of her scarf was trapped inside. *The People, 16 Dec 2007.*

MANFRED LUBITZ, 65, AN ELECTRICIAN from Berlin, died in his new home in Malaga, Spain, in 2003 while wired up to a homemade gadget. He told friends that his "orgasmatron" – named after a sex-machine in Woody Allen's film *Sleeper* – "was better than a woman and a lot cheaper". It had a vibrating mat, massage pads and electrodes to attach to his manhood. "Unfortunately there seems to have been a power surge while he was watching a film called *Hot Vixen Nuns*," said a police spokesman. "And the flat was damp." The cause of death was electrocution. *Glasgow Herald, 28 Mar 2003.*

A MAN DRESSED AS A KNIGHT FOR A mediæval jousting tournament died instantly when a bolt of lightning stuck his lance. The 51-year-old Swede was wearing full metal armour as part of an historical re-enactment near Stockholm. "There was steam coming from the eye slits of his helmet," said a witness. Two other men in armour were also hit and suffered severe burns. *D.Mail, 26 July 2006.*

CHAPTER 2

When Pets go Bad

Far from being man's best friend, a pet can often prove his deadliest enemy, as this selection of dangerous domesticated animals demonstrates...

DUCK-HUNTER THOMAS CHARLES, 28, WAS shot dead in January 2007 when his dog stood on his gun and it fired in Nashville, Tennessee. A month later, Dragos Mila, 37, was shot dead by a badger. He dropped his rifle when the animal fled a hole in Gornji Milanovac, Serbia. It then ran over the gun, which went off, shooting him in the stomach. *Sun, 16 Jan, 21 Feb; D.Record, 21 Feb 2007.*

A MONKEY THAT APPARENTLY TIRED OF BEING forced to climb palm trees killed its owner with a well-aimed coconut. Leilit Janchoom, 48, died immediately when the nut struck him in the Thai province of Nakorn Sri Thammarat. Janchoom received the equivalent of 4p for every coconut the monkey harvested from trees up to 50m (165ft) high. He regularly beat the animal whenever it showed any reluctance to climb. The monkey seemed to find the work boring, strenuous and unrewarding, according to the *Samui Express* newspaper. The victim's wife, Uthai, said they bought the monkey for about £130. "He seemed lovable," she said. "We called him Brother Kwan." *D.Mail, 11 Mar 2009.*

BENJI, A FRISKY FRENCH POODLE, KILLED his master by jumping into his lap as he was demonstrating the safety catch of a handgun to his mother, who was anxious about a spate of burglaries. The 30lb (14kg) poodle caused the gun to fire into his heart and John Hwilka, a 37-year-old former Marine, died within minutes of the accident. Benji licked Hwilka's face in a poignant effort to revive him. There were no plans to destroy the dog, which whined uncontrollably at his master's absence.

It was the second case in a fortnight of a dog killing its owner. Michael Trevethan, 42, of California, died after he got out of his pickup truck to open a gate and his dog put the vehicle into gear, crushing him against a post. The dog, a Rhodesian ridgeback, then died from dehydration because the truck's heater was set on full. From the cuts and bruises on Mr Trevethan's body, police deduced that he had struggled in vain to free himself, and may have been pinned for up to 15 hours before he died. *Guardian, 13 Sept, 16 Oct; NY Post. Eve. Standard, 15 Oct; Times, D.Post, D.Telegraph, 16 Oct 1998.*

PAMELA WEAVER WAS KILLED BY HER PET camel at her family's sheep and cattle ranch near the town of Mitchell in Queensland, Australia. It knocked her to the ground, stamped on her head, and lay on top of her. Husband Noel, who gave her the camel as a 60th birthday present in March 2006, returned home to discover her body on 18 August 2007. He had considered buying her a llama or alpaca, but found they were too expensive. The camel was just 10 months old, but already weighed 335lb (152kg) and had come close to suffocating the family's pet goat on a number of occasions. Mrs Weaver was in the middle of cooking dinner and there was a cup of tea on the kitchen table. The camel was wandering loose in the back yard.

Many reports said the camel was trying to mate with Mrs Weaver, but its behaviour was more consistent with seeing off a love rival. "What happened is certainly characteristic of a bull in season," said camel expert Paddy McHugh. "That's how they kill their opposition – they pull their legs out from underneath and then sit on them with their brisket, which is the hard bit underneath their chest."

Mr Weaver, who broke down in tears at his wife's funeral on 23 August, said: "You have to forgive the camel, he loved her very much. She loved animals, rearing everything from goats, kangaroos, emus, rabbits and the camel." The family agreed that the camel would not be destroyed. Chris Hill, who has been offering camel rides to tourists for

20 years, said camel calves were not aggressive, but could be dangerous if treated as pets. He had no doubt the camel's behaviour was sexual.

Though death by camel is extremely rare, there was another case only four months earlier. Cathie Ake, 55, who with her husband owned an exotic animal farm in Wewahitchka, Florida, died on 22 April after being kicked and then sat on by an 1,800lb (816kg) camel during a break in filming by a local television station. *[AAP] Metro, BBC News, 20 Aug; D.Mail, 20+25 Aug; (Sydney) D.Telegraph, 24 Aug 2007; Panama City News Herald, 24 April 2007.*

HELMUT OLPP, 51, DIED INSTANTLY on 16 August 1999 when both barrels of his shotgun were fired from the front seat of his car in a wood near the German spa town of Bad Urach during a hunting trip. The gun had gone off when his six-year-old Schwarzwi Oldbracke dog Bodo jumped on it. Forester Ulrich Meissner found the dog whimpering by the body. Only the victim's footprints and fingerprints were found, and suicide was ruled out because he was 15ft (4.6m) away from the gun. A spokesman said: "There was a smudge on the trigger which matched moisture from [the dog's] nose." Helmut's widow Regine, a mother-of-two, was going to keep Bodo. "He knows he will have to live with it, just as we will," she said. *[R] 19 Aug; D.Mail, D.Record, 20 Aug; Int. Express, 24 Aug 1999.*

FLATULENT PARROTS KILLED AN ANIMAL lover who collapsed and died in Tegelen, Holland. The unnamed victim, whose double-glazed house reeked of expelled wind from dozens of pet birds, had called an ambulance, saying he felt ill – but died before paramedics arrived. The police blamed a combination of the birds' farts and ammonia from their droppings. *Sun, 21 Nov 2003.*

CHAPTER 3

Twists of Fate

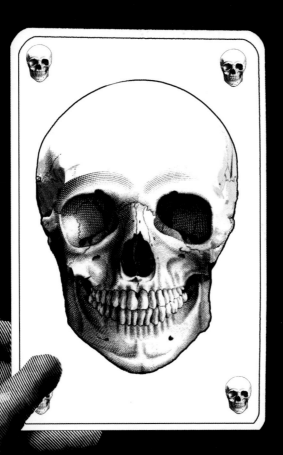

There are times when death seems to
be on the cards - and there's absolutely
nothing you can do to dodge the Grim Reaper...

GEORGE STORY FEATURED IN the inaugural issue of *Life* magazine 64 years ago as a newborn baby dangling by his feet. From that appearance, under the headline "Life Begins", he was known as "the *Life* Baby". As the magazine grew into an American institution, it continued to track its first star as he married twice, became a father and retired. He appeared in the magazine's final issue in May 2000, this time under the headline "A Life Ends". A few days after it was announced that the magazine was to fold, Mr Story died from heart failure. It was, as the article said, "sad and altogether strange". Man and magazine had been entwined. *Sunday Telegraph, 21 May 2000.*

A THIEF DIED TRYING to flee an art museum in Bonn. Peter Gruber panicked after being surprised by a security guard at the Klausmann Museum of Art and when he raced round a corner, impaled himself upon a 4ft (1.2m)-long sword held by a statue of a blindfolded soldier. The exhibit is called "The Weapon of Justice". *Guardian, 29 June 2000.*

LOUIS DETHY, 79, A FORMER CHEMICAL engineer who booby-trapped his house in Belgium with the intention of killing his estranged family, died himself in 2002 when he inadvertently triggered one of his own devices. He had built the three-storey brick and timber house in Pont-de-Loup, near Charleroi, in the 1960s, on land belonging to and with materials paid for by his mother. When his wife caught him in bed with another woman in the 1980s, she walked out, taking their children with her.

Dethy became a recluse, and never forgave his 10 daughters, four sons and 37 grandchildren for having little to do with him. When his own mother turned against him, she bequeathed the property to one of his

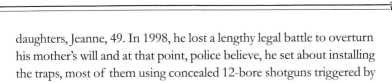

daughters, Jeanne, 49. In 1998, he lost a lengthy legal battle to overturn his mother's will and at that point, police believe, he set about installing the traps, most of them using concealed 12-bore shotguns triggered by barely-visible nylon threads or fishing line.

Following his death, military mine-clearance experts uncovered many traps, among them an apparently harmless but lethal pile of dinner plates, a chest in the cellar full of money, and even an exploding crate of beer. Other shotguns were found wired to the television, a water tank and the bathroom door. Dethy had numbered and catalogued each device and left coded notes for the whereabouts of each.

It took three weeks to crack 19 of the 20 clues, but after taking the house apart the experts were forced to admit defeat on the final one: "The 12 Apostles are ready to work on the pebbles". They concluded that Dethy had not yet put it in place. Device number 18, the one that killed him – which he had either failed, or forgotten, to disarm – was hidden in the kitchen dresser and triggered by moving a soup tureen. "Father was a strange, cold man," said his daughter Jeanne. "He wanted to kill us all." *D. Telegraph, 10 Nov 2002.*

 A 75-YEAR-OLD MAN DIED AFTER accidentally triggering a booby trap he had set up in his house near Quebec City. Jos Lawrence Potvin had rigged a rifle to a string that ran across the floor of his bedroom to project his home from thieves. The police found his body on 21 October 2010. It appeared he had been preparing a meal when he set off the trap by mistake. *[CP] (Toronto) Globe and Mail, 23 Oct 2010.*

A FACTORY OWNER WITH MONEY TROUBLES climbed on the roof of his building in central Thailand to raise a flag believed to ward off bad luck – then slipped and fell to his death. Boonchai Lotharakphong, 43, whose factory made sportswear for Nike, died when he slipped off the roof in Lopburi province, 70 miles (113km) north of Bangkok. He had been sold the flag by a Chinese fortune-teller. *[AP] 15 Nov 2003.*

CARISSA GLENN, 18, FOUND HANGING BY A pink scarf from a shower rail in her flat in St Ives, Cornwall, in April 2008, might have killed herself while sleepwalking after becoming haunted by a rumour that a woman had hanged herself in the flat before she moved in – a rumour that turned out to be false. Miss Glenn, a barmaid known to her friends as Tish, was a talented pianist, artist and rider, but had a history of sleepwalking episodes in which she acted out her dreams. "She was always spooked by the supernatural," said her sister Lara. "She believed there was a presence in the flat and would mention it two or three times a week. She was always talking about her dreams – they were vivid. She must have been asleep or half-conscious." Her mother Lusia said: "She would never have deliberately taken her own life." An inquest in Truro in November 2008 recorded an open verdict. *D.Telegraph, D.Mail, 1 Nov 2008.*

A MAN SEARCHING FOR A LEGENDARY GHOST train was killed when a real locomotive came down the tracks and hit him. Christopher Kaiser, 29, of Charlotte had gathered with around 12 others on the anniversary of a crash that happened near Statesville, North Carolina, at 3am on 27 August 1891, when seven carriages fell off the Bostian Bridge into a ravine and 30 people died. According to local legend, the sounds of the accident, including the train whistle, screeching wheels, and the screams of passengers, can be heard again on the anniversary and each year people go to listen. It is also claimed that people have seen a uniformed man with a gold watch. On the centenary of the crash in 1991, more than 150 people turned up.

At 2.45am on the anniversary in 2010, Kaiser was waiting on a trestle near the site of the old Bostian Bridge, off Buffalo Shoals Road, when the real train came round a bend. The ghost-hunters began running along the trestle and most of them made it the 150ft (45m) to safety. Kaiser pushed a woman with him to safety. She fell at least 30ft (9m) and was being treated for injuries. Kaiser's body was found under the trestle in a deep ravine. WCNC.com, 27 Aug; *dailymail.co.uk, 29 Aug; telegraph. co.uk, 30 Aug 2010.*

NAJIB KHOURY, A THRIFTY SYRIAN, stashed his life savings of £15,000 in a box, which he placed in a hole in the wall. Then he dreamed that he had given all his money to charity. He rushed to check his hiding place and found a family of mice nesting in the box, which was comfortably lined with chewed-up banknotes. Mr Khoury had a heart attack and dropped dead. *D. Express, 25 Sept 1999.*

THE FULLY CLOTHED SKELETON OF a would-be burglar was found on 19 January 2001, lodged in the chimney of the Riverboat Gift Shop in the historic district of Natchez, Mississippi, during renovation work, solving the case of a man who disappeared nearly 16 years earlier. Police conjectured that Calvin Wilson, 27 at the time of his disappearance in 1985, fell headfirst down the chimney, was injured and could not call for help. The remains were identified by pay stubs and jewellery.

A man's decomposed body was discovered in a duct at the Magna

Tools manufacturing plant in Racine, Wisconsin, when an access panel was opened on 23 February 2001. It was thought that he had got stuck there during a robbery attempt the previous November. *[AP] 24 Jan, 3 Mar; Shreveport (LA) Times, 26 Jan 2001.*

THAN SINGH, 70, A DAIRY FARMER IN northeast India, was left aghast after receiving a bogus receipt for his own cremation service a week earlier. He complained of chest pains and was rushed to hospital, but suffered a massive heart attack and died. His body was then delivered to the same crematorium in Ghaziabad that was mentioned in the mysterious letter. In a further macabre twist, the body was issued with the same serial number – 89. Suspicious relatives called in police, who believe the death was the result of a prank rather than an administrative mistake. "The element of mischief is apparent and obvious," said Raghubir Lal, senior superintendent of police in Ghaziabad. "What remains to be deciphered is if the person behind it wanted to shock the old man to the extent that he might collapse and if so then why, or if it was merely a prank that took a serious turn." *Newscore, via www.news.com. au, 26 June 2010.*

A TENPIN BOWLER COLLAPSED AND DIED on 30 December 2005 at a bowling alley in Michigan shortly after rolling the third perfect game of his life. Ed Lorenz, 69, bowled a 300 – the highest possible score – in his first league game of the night at Airway Lanes in the town of Portage. When he got up to bowl in the fifth frame of his second game, he clutched his chest and fell over, and efforts to revive him failed. "If he could have written a way to go out, this would be it," said Johnny Masters, who was bowling with Lorenz.

Another tenpin bowler in Michigan collapsed and died after recording

his first perfect score in October 2008. Don Doane, 62, belonged to the same bowling team for 45 years and finally managed to rack up the maximum 300. As he was high-fiving his teammates, he collapsed on the floor with a heart attack and died in hospital. *Irish Examiner, Northern Territory News, 31 Dec 2005; Irish Independent, 1 Nov 2008.*

HERNAN HERRARA, 36, SURVIVED A CRASH into a tree in Miami Beach, Florida, on 17 January 1999, but died when he got out of his car and was hit be a utility pole. Police think that he was warning other drivers of the downed electrical wires when another car hit the dangling lines, causing the pole to snap. *[AP] 19 Jan 1999.*

GERMAN TOURIST HERMANN ROAG somehow survived a fall from the window of his 8th floor hotel room in Lausanne, Switzerland, with no more than a broken ankle; but on the way to hospital he fell out of the ambulance and died under the wheels of a passing bus. *Guardian, 23 Nov 2000.*

JENNY RIDER, 41, POURED PETROL OVER her clothes and set it alight. As it flared, she changed her mind and plunged into a river in new Norfolk, Tasmania, to douse the flames. She then knocked herself unconscious on a rock and drowned. *News of the World, 24 Sept 2000.*

GERMAN TOURIST ISABEL VON JORDAN, 25, was in the Sari nightclub in Bali an hour before the explosion that killed at least 191 people on 12 October 2002. She then travelled to Australia with her sister to visit friends hurt in the explosion, but the Grim Reaper had marked her card. On 23 October, her body was pulled from the jaws of a 13ft (3.9m) crocodile in the northern Australian outback after she took a late night swim in the Sandy Billabong waterhole in Kakadu National Park. *D.Mail, 24 Oct; Ananova, 25 Oct 2002.*

COLLEGE STUDENT JUSTIN PARKER, 24, OF Ames, Iowa, survived after his car went down a steep embankment near Red Cliff, Colorado, around 25 September 2007. The car was spotted the next day. It had plunged about 300ft (90m), landing upright. There were foot-steps leading from the car and disappearing over another cliff. Parker's body was found at the base of that cliff. *Rocky Mountain News, 10 Oct 2007.*

A NEW DELHI LABOURER SURVIVED GETTING hit by a bus, only to get hit and killed by a second bus 20 minutes later. Raj Kumar, 38, was on his way to work on New Year's Eve 2008 when a bus hit him from behind. Local residents took the injured man to the hospital inside a three-wheeler taxi. Before they reached the hospital, however, Mr Kumar said he felt fine and jumped out of the vehicle to cross the road – but another bus hit him and he died on the spot. Both vehicles were Blueline buses, infamous for running red lights and speed-ing through the city's free-for-all traffic. The *Hindustan Times* said Blueline buses caused 118 deaths in 2008. *[PA] 1 Jan; (Sydney) D.Telegraph, 2 Jan 2009.*

CHAPTER 4

Strange Suicides

Taking one's own life is a tragic business, but some suicides display an impressive level of inventiveness, while other cries for help are sadly ignored...

LIFT ENGINEER JAMES RAYNOR, 61, OF Netherhall, Leicester, tied a noose to the top of an elevator shaft, stood on the lift roof and waited patiently in the dark for it to go down. He was killed when the lift was called to a lower floor. He was depressed after losing his driving licence for driving while drunk. *D.Mirror, 12 Mar 1998.*

A CHEERFUL MAN KILLED HIMSELF so that he could avoid losing his feelings of happiness. Syrian police said Najib Saddi, 35, the boss of a fish firm, left a suicide note saying he was "perfectly happy" but was afraid of "future unhappiness". *D.Express, 29 April 2000.*

A ROMANIAN MAN WHO wanted to kill himself had a heart attack before being able to hang himself from a rope he had tied to the ceiling. Iosif Capota wrote farewell notes, then locked himself in a Calimanesti hotel room. The rope was hanging nearby. *(London) Eve. Standard, 13 Sept 2000.*

THE BADLY CHARRED BODY OF DANIEL McMillan, 37, was found in dense woodland in the Edinburgh suburb of Granton on 20 July 2004. Detectives believe that he dug himself a shallow grave in the grounds of derelict Muirhouse Mansion near his home. Standing inside the hole, he evidently soaked himself in petrol and then handcuffed himself. He then lay down, pulled a metal lid over the grave, set fire to himself and burned to death in his DIY furnace. The body was discovered ablaze by police officers on routine patrol. *Edinburgh Eve. News, 21+22+23+29+30 July 2004.*

A CULT MEMBER POISONED HIMSELF BY eating yew tree leaves in a New Age suicide ritual, an inquest heard on 14 October 2005. Stephen Davidson, 35, a member of the Barry Long Foundation, died alone in Butleigh Woods near his home in Glastonbury, Somerset, the previous April. He was found by a passer-by near a pile of yew tree leaves, healing crystals, pebbles and a book called *The Ending of Time*. His tent, pitched nearby, was painted with occult images, many of a sexual nature. He had tiny particles of leaf in his throat, resulting in yew leaf toxicity: fatal breathing and heart problems. He had been living in the woods for more than a week before his body was found. *Independent, 15 Oct 2005.*

A MAN IS THOUGHT TO HAVE COMMITTED suicide in June 2006 by tying himself to a ladder on a Thames jetty at Convoy's Wharf in Deptford, and waiting to be drowned by the rising tide. Police found no evidence of foul play. *(London) Eve. Standard, 23 June 2006.*

A MAN INTENT ON SUICIDE TIED A 25ft (7.6m) plastic drainpipe to an electricity pylon near a park-and-ride in Botley, Oxfordshire, on 12 December 2006 and suspended a carving knife from the top of the pipe with a rope. Then he sat below the homemade 'guillotine' and let go of the rope, sending the heavy knife plunging through his skull. "It is one of the most elaborate and bizarre suicides we have dealt with," said a Thames Valley Police source. "It must have been an incredibly painful death." The dead man was in his early to mid-twenties, white, slim with short brown hair, and about 5ft 11ins (180cm) tall. Detectives were unable to match him with any missing person. *Sun, 14 Dec 2006.*

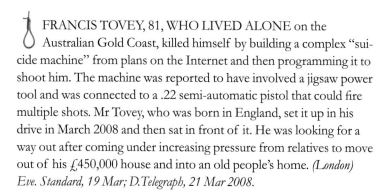

FRANCIS TOVEY, 81, WHO LIVED ALONE on the
Australian Gold Coast, killed himself by building a complex "suicide machine" from plans on the Internet and then programming it to shoot him. The machine was reported to have involved a jigsaw power tool and was connected to a .22 semi-automatic pistol that could fire multiple shots. Mr Tovey, who was born in England, set it up in his drive in March 2008 and then sat in front of it. He was looking for a way out after coming under increasing pressure from relatives to move out of his £450,000 house and into an old people's home. *(London) Eve. Standard, 19 Mar; D.Telegraph, 21 Mar 2008.*

WINDOW CLEANER JEFFREY BURTON, 57, died after
stabbing himself repeatedly in the groin with a jumbo souvenir pencil. Police found his body is a blood-soaked room in his house in St Leonards, East Sussex, on 27 September 2009. He was lying on his back, wearing only his underpants, with the giant, blood-covered pencil beside him. "It seems to me that it can't have been a single stab wound," said East Sussex coroner Alan Craze. "He seems to have worked on it. The pencil was blunt." Mr Burton's sister told the inquest the pencil had sentimental value to her brother as it had once belonged to their late mother, and he had used it in "yoga-like exercises". *D.Mirror, 6 Mar; Brighton Argus, 9 Mar 2010.*

RENATO DI PAOLO, 23, HANGED himself on 22 April
2000 during an Easter Passion play in Camerata Nuova, a hamlet of 200 people 47 miles (75km) from Rome, while portraying Judas Iscariot, the apostle who betrayed Jesus and then committed suicide in remorse. It was 10 minutes before the audience and his fellow actors realised that Di Paolo wasn't acting but was unconscious after the

noose, lashed to a tree branch, pulled tightly around his neck. He was rushed to a hospital, where he was pronounced dead. *[AP] 23 April 2000.*

WHEN PAUL LUDWIG, 69, COMMITTED suicide in the summer of 1980, he didn't want his family to find his body. Suffering from cancer, he left a note at home saying: "Don't look for me – you won't find me." He then climbed a tree, tied himself to it and shot himself with a rifle (or pistol), which he'd lashed to his body to stop it falling to the ground. There he stayed for 29 years, concealed by thick branches and leaves, until Sebastian Gunther and Stefanie Bauer, both 20, (or, alternatively, a lone, unnamed 18-year-old hiker), found a bone in the bushes and notified the police in April 2009. Officers entered the woods and found a hip fitted with two artificial joints. Looking up, they discovered the skeleton 11m (36ft) above them in a fir tree in Bruckberg, southern Germany. "With two artificial hips, I've no idea how he managed to climb up the tree. It wasn't so high, I guess, 30 years ago," said Mr Ludwig's nephew, Klaus Kiefl, 39. Police believe the rope got tighter as the tree grew and eventually severed the arm and leg bones, which fell to the ground. *[R] Metro, 7 April 2009.*

THE APPARENT SUICIDE OF A WOMAN FOUND hanged in a tree was ignored for hours because passers-by thought she was a Hallowe'en decoration. The 42-year-old woman's body was suspended 15ft (5m) from the ground at the side of a busy road in Frederica, Delaware, on the night of 25 October 2005. Neighbours noticed the body at breakfast time the next morning, but dismissed it

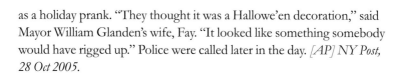

as a holiday prank. "They thought it was a Hallowe'en decoration," said Mayor William Glanden's wife, Fay. "It looked like something somebody would have rigged up." Police were called later in the day. *[AP] NY Post, 28 Oct 2005.*

THE DEATH OF AN ARTIST WHO JUMPED from the fifth floor of Tacheles, an alternative cultural centre in Berlin, on 4 December 2002 was interpreted as performance art by passers-by. Instead of calling an ambulance, they took pictures. Many thought her body, seeping blood, was a clever doll, a preview of an exhibition due to open the following day, which included work by the dead artist. The 24-year-old woman, identified only as Janine F, was part of Berlin's "Manufactur" art group and was known for her cardboard sculptures. The night before her suicide, she told her fellow-artists of her intentions, but they didn't take her seriously, and began filming her with a video camera. Tacheles had a reputation for avant garde art. The bombed-out building, once a department store and exhibition hall, had been home to an anarchic artist collective for decades. *Irish Times, 6 Dec 2002.*

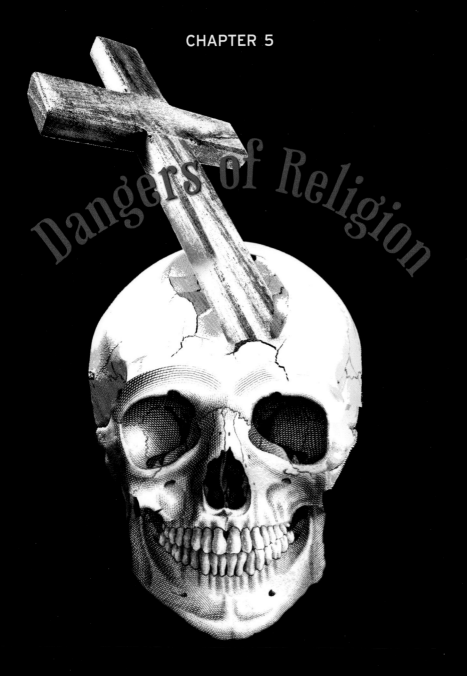

CHAPTER 5

Dangers of Religion

Religious faith is no protection against the end that awaits us all. In fact, it sometimes appears to hasten some very unusual departures...

FIVE BUDDHIST WORSHIPPERS WERE killed on 2 November 1998 when three giant ceremonial joss sticks collapsed at one of Thailand's most sacred sites, the Phra Pathom Jedi temple 36 miles (58km) north-west of Bangkok. The 79ft-88ft (24-27m) tall joss sticks, said to be the largest ever built in Thailand, crumbled under their own weight, possibly because they were soaked by heavy overnight rain, though the police blamed inadequate foundations. The victims were among more than 1,000 Buddhists attending a ceremony at the temple. The joss sticks, built the previous April to commemorate the 84th anniversary of the construction of a Buddha image at the temple, were made from thousands of smaller joss sticks bundled together on a wire frame. *[R] Bangkok Post, D.Telegraph, 3 Nov 1998.*

THREE CULT MEMBERS FROM SUKMAJAYA, east Java, were beaten to death by fellow cultists when the 9.9.99 dooms-day prediction failed to materialise. Like many cults across Indonesia, members were told to prepare for the end of the world at 9am on 9 September. They sold their possessions and locked themselves up in their homes for the preceding nine days. *[R] 13 Sept 1999.*

THE BADLY DECOMPOSED BODIES of Suiko Wakasa (41), her sisters Kaoru (38), Eiko (29), and Hiromi (28), and brother Minoru (27), were found in their home in Osaka, western Japan, on 16 August 2000 by police who forced their way into the house after a call from a worried relative. The siblings were found side by side on futons in two rooms and were thought to have died from starvation about a month earlier. "Some of the faces were beyond recognition. The bodies were covered with maggots and flies," said a policeman.

Their mother Akiko (64) and uncle, Takao Wakasa (66), both suffering from malnutrition, were questioned by police. The mother said her children died after the uncle told them not to eat in a "divine instruction" to remove impurities. They lasted four weeks without food. The family had played religious music all day and spread large quantities of salt outside the house. They covered their windows with corrugated iron and dug four circular holes 7ft (2m) deep in the garden, which the mother said were to "allow God to breathe". *[AFP] D.Telegraph, 18 Aug; Guardian, 19 Aug 2000.*

THE REV JACK ARNOLD, 69, WAS NEARING the end of his sermon at Covenant Presbyterian Church in Oviedo, a suburb of Orlando, Florida, on 9 January 2005 when he collapsed and died in mid-sentence. Arnold quoted John Wesley, who said: "Until my work on this Earth is done, I am immortal. But when my work for Christ is done... I go to be with Jesus…" whereupon he grabbed the podium and fell to the floor. *[AP] 10 Jan 2005.*

JOSIP LONZA, 62, WAS LEADING A FUNERAL procession in Brezovica, near the Slovenian capital Ljubljana, carrying a large metal cross, when the cross was hit by lightning. Mourners were scattered and Lonza struck dead. *D.Express, 25 May 2005.*

VIDYAWATI SINGH, 35, THREW HERSELF into the flames of her husband's funeral pyre in May 2006 as 400 people watched in Rari Bujurg, a village in the Fatehpur district of Uttar Pradesh. She was dead within minutes, leaving behind three children. According to the superintendent of the nearest police station, Lakhan Singh's family blamed his widow for his death because the couple had not been getting on, and made her feel that her life would be so dishonourable that she would be better off committing sati. Police arrested more than a dozen villagers, including three of her brothers-in-law. A month ealier, Sita Devi, 78, died on her husband's pyre in Bihar, eastern India.

Sati (or suttee) was outlawed in 1831 by Lord Bentinck, the Governor-General of India, but it continues in certain rural areas. "Often it's because no one wants to bother looking after an old widow, or her family want to grab the dead husband's property," said Girija Vyas, the chairwoman of the National Commission for Women. The Indian government was under pressure to pass new legislation making it possible to prosecute whole communities for failing to prevent the practice, but collective punishment would set a dangerous precedent. As it stood, the law prescribed a life sentence or death for anyone convicted of abetting sati, but convictions were hard to secure because villagers refuse to bear witness. *Scotsman, 25 April; Times, 23 May 2006.*

THE DEATH OF A TERMINALLY ILL WOMAN who performed the Jain rite of santhara or "fasting unto death" stirred fierce debate in India over whether the 1,000-year-old practice is still appropriate. Vimla Devi Bhansali, 61, suffering from cancer of the brain and liver, refused food and water from 14 September 2006 and died on the 28th in the city of Jaipur in Rajasthan as the state high court was considering a petition by a human rights campaigner trying to stop the fast. Hundreds came to Mrs Bhansali's home to pay their respects to a woman now considered to have attained moksha, or the realisation of the soul's true nature. Her body, dressed in a colourful sari and held in a sitting position, was paraded through packed streets to the cremation ground.

Social welfare groups compare santhara to suicide, euthanasia and sati.

Jains insist that those who oppose santhara fail to understand its motivation. A Jain spokesman explained that the ritual "is taken up by someone who has performed all his duties and wants to purify the soul before leaving the world." Subjects have ample time to reconsider their position and are free to eat at any time. Although there are only 15 million Jains worldwide, the religion has profoundly shaped thought in Southeast Asia. Jains make up some of the most literate and prosperous communities in India. *Guardian, 30 Sept; D.Telegraph, 2 Oct 2006.*

✝ ON 4 JANUARY 2007, THREE MEN IN the western Chinese province of Shaanxi were arrested for killing two young women to sell their corpses as "ghost brides" for dead single men, a custom known as *minghun,* dating back to before the Han dynasty. In the yellow-earth highlands of western China, there is a belief that young men and women who die unmarried should go to their graves accompanied by a recently deceased partner to be their spouse in the afterlife. It is thought that the unmarried dead will often haunt the living in dreams and can ruin the prosperity of future generations.

Yang Donghai, 35-year-old peasant, confessed to killing a woman bought from a poor family for 12,000 yuan (£785) in 2006. Yang said he was "tricked" into buying the girl, who was mentally handicapped and unable to care for herself. Realising she was not marriage material for himself, Yang hatched a plan to recover his losses with Liu Shengha. They made contact with "Old Li", Li Longsheng, an undertaker in Xixian county known for trading dead women for "ghost weddings". Yang and Liu poisoned and then strangled the girl, selling the corpse to Li for 16,000 yuan. Emboldened by their success, Yang and Liu, with help from Hui Haibao, lured a prostitute to an abandoned courtyard in the city of Yan'an where they strangled her and sold her to Li on 3 December for 8,000 yuan. "It's a good thing we broke the case when we did, otherwise who knows how many women would have been murdered? These guys found a get-rich-quick scheme," said the chief of police in Yangchuan county. *[R,AP] 25 Jan; Times, Scotsman, 26 Jan 2007.*

MOSCOW POLICE BROKE INTO THE FLAT of the Komarov family in Artyukhino Road in the south-west of the city in 2005 after complaints that they had not paid their utility bills for months. They found the mummified bodies of a man and three women. The flat was full of icons and Russian Orthodox devotional literature. There was no sign of a disturbance. An initial examination showed that the owner of the flat, Timofie Komarov, born in 1912, had died about 10 years earlier. His body was found on a bed, a calendar above his head opened on the year 1997. His wife, Anna Komarova (born 1914) was found in a separate room, also on a bed. She had died at least three years earlier. Their daughter, Alla Ivkina (born 1942) and her daughter Anna Ivkina (born 1971) lay in the kitchen. These two had died about two years earlier.

"As the bodies are mummified, it is impossible [immediately] to determine the cause of death," said Sergei Marchenko, a spokesman for the Moscow prosecutor's office. "We will be able to speak about this after the chemical and DNA tests on the remains." A source close to the investigation told the RIA Novosti news agency that the family could have been part of a "non-established sect" that "poisoned themselves during a ritual". The source said that two bottles containing a dark residue had been found and were being tested. *Guardian, 9 June 2005.*

CHAPTER 6

Out with a Bang!

Messing about with hand grenades is never a good
idea, but anything from mobile phones to chewing
gum can lead to a literally explosive exit...

OUT WITH A BANG!

ALBERTO ALVADOROS, 34, EXPLODED AND died as surgeons in Guayaquil, Ecuador, used a scalpel to open him up. Heat from the instrument ignited methane in his gut, causing a ball of flame. Operating staff suffered minor injuries and shock. *Sun, 7 Mar 1998.*

MOUV NGET, A 36-YEAR-OLD CAMBODIAN man, became angry when fellow revellers at a party in Sampouv Loeun accused him of being a ghost and not a real man. He left the party and returned with a stick and then a knife. After being thrown out both times, he went home and returned with a Chinese hand grenade "to prove he was alive"; but the grenade accidentally blew up in his hand, killing him and seriously wounding five others. Perhaps he was able to attend a subsequent party as a *real* ghost… *Canberra Times, 11 Dec 2005.*

A BRAZILIAN MAN DIED WHEN HE TRIED to open what police believe was a rocket-propelled grenade – with a sledgehammer. Another man suffered severe burns after the grenade exploded in a workshop on the outskirts of Rio de Janeiro. The blast destroyed the workshop and left several cars in flames. Police believe the ammunition was brought to the men by scavengers wanting to sell it as scrap metal. *D.Mail, 10 Aug 2006.*

A CAMBODIAN MAN ACCIDENTALLY BLEW himself up while threatening his wife with a hand grenade to shut her up. Pen Pheng, the police chief of the southeastern province of Prey

Veng, said Chaeng Kim Hoan, 41, a former soldier, frequently fought with his wife, Mam Pen Sreng. The wife was not injured in the explosion. *Brisbane Courier-Mail, 15 June 2006.*

WELDER XIAO JINPENG WAS WORKING AT THE Yingpan Iron Ore Dressing Plant in Gansu's Jinta county in western China in 2007 when a Motorola cell phone in his chest pocket exploded, breaking some of his ribs, and his heart was pierced by fragments of bone. He died at a local hospital. A government inquiry said the phone's lithium battery had exploded due to heat at the mill where he was working. In Guangdong province – one of the world's biggest electronics manufacturing centres – officials said they had found batteries in Motorola and Nokia mobiles that failed safety tests and were prone to explode under certain conditions. Motorola and Nokia denied the link, suggesting the batteries were counterfeit.

A shopworker in Guangzhou, China, died on 30 January 2009 when the cell phone in his chest pocket exploded, severing a major artery in his neck. The make and model of the phone were not known. A computer shop employee heard a bang and saw her 20-year-old colleague lying on the floor in a pool of blood. She said the man had recently swapped his mobile phone battery for a new one. This was the ninth recorded cell phone explosion in China since 2002. *(London) Eve. Standard, 4 July; Western Mail, 5 July 2007; The Register, 3 Feb; D.Mail, 4 Feb 2009.*

AN UNNAMED "BLACK WIDOW" SUICIDE bomber, who planned a terrorist attack near Red Square in Moscow on New Year's Eve 2010, was killed when an unexpected text message set off her bomb too early, according to Russian security services. They believe that a spam message from her cell phone operator wishing her a Happy New Year received hours before the planned attack triggered her suicide belt, killing her at a safe house. She was thought to be part of the same group that struck Moscow's Domodedovo airport on 24 January 2011. Islamist terrorists in Russia often use new cell phones as detonators. They are usually kept switched off until the last moment, but in this case the terrorist was evidently careless. *D.Telegraph, 27 Jan 2011.*

A CHEMISTRY STUDENT FROM UKRAINE was killed by exploding chewing gum on 5 December 2009. Vladimir Likhonos, 25, a student at a regional branch of the Kiev Polytechnic Institute, was working at a computer in his parents' house in the northern city of Konotop when relatives heard what was described as 'a loud pop', and rushed into his room. They discovered that the lower half of his face had been blown off. Medical workers who arrived on the scene attempted to treat his injuries but were unable to save him. It transpired that Likhonos had a bizarre habit of dipping his chewing gum in citric acid to give it a sour taste (or prolong the taste – reports differ), said police spokeswoman Elvira Biganova. On his table, police found both citric acid packets and about 100g of a similar-looking unidentified substance, believed to be some kind of explosive. Investigators believe he simply confused the packets and put the gum covered with explosive material into his mouth. At the time of the report, authorities were waiting on the results of further tests to identify the mystery substance. *Ria Novosti news agency (Moscow), 8 Dec; Sun, 10 Dec; (Dublin) Metro, 11 Dec 2009.*

CHAPTER 7

Joint Exits

"Till death do us part" goes the marriage vow, and some couples really don't seem able to live without one another...

ARTHUR AUDETTE, 84, AND HIS WIFE LORETTA, 77, died within 10 minutes of each other in Pawtucket, Rhode Island, on 12 December 1996 – their 54th wedding anniversary. They were married in Atlantic City, New Jersey, in 1942. Both were patients at Memorial Hospital, which didn't give the causes of their deaths. *[AP] 14 Dec 1996.*

A COUPLE MARRIED FOR 50 YEARS DIED WITHIN seven minutes of each other in the same hospital after suffering heart attacks in 1997. The family of Colin and Joan Beaumont, both 74, said they couldn't live without each other. Mr Beaumont was taken ill at the wheel on the way to see his wife at the Kent and Canterbury Hospital. *Sun, D.Express, 13 June 1997.*

ALEC KELLAS, 89, AND HIS WIFE ALICE, 88 – married for 68 years – died almost simultaneously from natural causes at their home in Keith, Scotland, on 26 November 2000. One died after an unspecified illness and the other had a heart attack. *Aberdeen Eve. News, 27 Nov 2000.*

DWAYNE CARROLL, 48, FROM KENTUCKY, had a fatal heart attack in July 2001 while clearing a place for the double gravestone intended to commemorate himself and his wife in the Floyd County cemetery. When he was late arriving home, his wife Carolyn, 49, sent her sister, Shelby Shrewsberry, to look for him. Mrs Carroll had a fatal heart attack herself when her sister told her the news. The headstone had the names and birth dates of both husband and wife on it, but only one date of death was required. There was to be a joint funeral service. *Ananova, 11 July 2001.*

LEONARD PLATTS, 82, AND HIS WIFE PEARL, 80, had been inseparable since their marriage in 1940. Mr Platts died in hospital on 22 November 2002. Minutes later, his wife died in her sleep at their home in Leicester. *D.Express, 26 Nov 2002.*

AFTER 63 YEARS OF MARRIAGE, HELEN AND Bill Wilson died within a day of each other. Bill was 94, Helen 92. They met as teenagers in Qualicum, British Columbia, in the 1920s, but didn't marry until 1940. Bill later became president of the Canadian Ophthalmological Society. They retired to Qualicum Beach in 1979, and moved into a care home in April 2003. Bill fell ill with flu and was taken to hospital in Nanaimo on 19 December 2003. That night, as Helen spoke to her son Jack, she began referring to her husband in the past tense and talked about how much she would miss him. Six hours later, she died in her sleep. In the morning, Jack visited his father in hospital. Finding him slightly delirious, he kept back the news of Helen's death and talked about other things. "At one point he said to me, 'Jack, get a chair for your mother'. I said, 'Why?' He said, 'She's standing in the doorway.'" Jack never did tell his father that Helen had died. The next day, Bill Wilson was gone too. *Victoria (BC) Times-Colonist, 27 Dec 2003.*

WILLIAM TRUMAN, 62, SUFFERED A STROKE while pilot-ing his single-engine plane from Laconia, New Hampshire, less than 15 minutes into the flight to Utica, New York, on 9 August 2004. Moments later, his wife Diane, 60, also suffered a stroke. Their daughter Jennifer took over the controls and made a safe landing in Laconia with help from an air traffic controller. Her parents were taken to hospital. Diane never regained consciousness and was taken off life support on 22 August. Her husband was semi-conscious but disoriented when he was taken to the hospital and suffered another stroke that killed him the day before his wife died. *[AP] Lebanon Valley (NH) News, 25 Aug 2004.*

DR MARVIN HERZOG AND HIS WIFE, DR Bernice 'Toots' Herzog, worked together as optometrists in Whitehall, Pennsylvania, for 45 years; they had been married for over 50 years. On 4 January 2007, upon learning that his wife's cancer was terminal, Dr Herzog had a fatal heart attack, an hour before his wife died. He was 89; she was 87. Their son Jeffrey explained that his mother's nickname, 'Toots', had been given her as a child by her uncles, the Three Stooges. "My father idolised my mother," he said. "They spent every hour of every day with each other. He could not live without her. When he found out her illness was terminal, he just folded his cards." *Pittsburgh Post-Gazette, 5 Jan 2007.*

PAT FISHER, 77, WAS DIAGNOSED WITH CANCER and was taken to hospital in Melbourne, where she died unexpectedly. Hospital staff rang her husband Arthur on 14 May 2007 and left a message for him to contact them. When he failed to return their call, they got the local police to investigate. They discovered that Arthur, 78, had died of a heart attack at about the same time as his wife. He had a kidney complaint, but it wasn't considered life-threatening. The couple had been inseparable throughout 55 years of marriage. "We really believe that they literally couldn't live without each other," said daughter Lynette Court. *Melbourne Herald Sun, 18 May 2007.*

BRIAN ECKERSLEY, 72, A RETIRED INSURANCE clerk from Radcliffe, near Bury, had adored his wife Betty, a factory

worker, since he met her at a Manchester dance hall. They celebrated their 50th wedding anniversary on 22 June 2007, but decided on a holiday in Majorca with their daughter and two grandchildren as a way of prolonging the festivities. Just before they were due to travel home, Mrs Eckersley suffered a brain hæmorrhage. In hospital she was placed on a life support machine. Her husband suffered a fatal heart attack the next morning as he kept vigil by his wife's bedside. Hours later, the life-support machine aiding his wife's breathing was turned off. "In all the days they were married my parents had not spent a day apart," said their daughter, Carol Cutler. "They died on the same day, which was also my father's birthday. He simply could not live without her." *Times, Sun, 21 July 2007.*

JOAN STANDEN, 84, FROM PAULSGROVE, Hampshire, was rushed to Southampton General Hospital with a chest infection and soon fell into a coma with pneumonia. Four days later, her husband Reg, 87, was taken to hospital with a similar condition. Joan died later that day at 2pm and Reg five hours later – even though his family had not told him about his wife's death because they thought him too weak. The couple were buried together on 1 February 2007 – their 66th wedding anniversary. "They were devoted to each other all those years, only ever separated by war or sickness," said their daughter, Melody Robbins. *The News (Portsmouth), 22 Jan; Sun, 23 Jan 2007.*

IN ALMOST 71 YEARS OF MARRIAGE, Jack and Helen Hope always said that each would not be able to go on living without the other. They met when Mr Hope was delivering meat in a horse-drawn cart for a butcher in Happisburgh, Norfolk, and romance blossomed at a village dance in 1930. They were married in Sea Pelling, Norfolk, on 22 April 1935 and lived in the area for most of their lives. In September 2004 they moved from sheltered accommodation in Norwich to live with their daughter Angela Pratt, 61, and her husband in Nacton, Suffolk.

Mrs Hope, 94, was admitted to Ipswich Hospital at the end of February 2006, when she was diagnosed with pneumonia. Mr Hope, 98, was taken to visit his wife, but she was too ill even to open her eyes or speak to him. He collapsed the following day and was also admitted to the hospital, where he died of a brain haemorrhage 15 hours later. "They hadn't spent a night apart until he went into hospital for a minor operation some years ago," said Mrs Pratt. "He realised mum wasn't going to get better. The death certificate may say the cause of death was a brain hæmorrhage, but I think he died of a broken heart." *D.Mail, 10 Mar 2006.*

A COUPLE IN IDLEB, NORTHWEST SYRIA, DIED on the same day in January 2008 after living together for more than 70 years. The husband, who was 95, died just hours after his 90-year-old wife had passed away. They left 66 grandchildren and great grandchildren. *[RIA Novosti] 15 Jan 2008.*

KENT AND DIANA KRAFT OF SIOUX FALLS, South Dakota, died together on 9 February 2008, side by side, of separate illnesses. Mrs Kraft had Lou Gehrig's Disease and her husband had a heart condition. They had both been born on 2 September 1941 and had been married for about 43 years. *Sioux Falls Argus Leader, 13 Feb 2008.*

CHAPTER 8

A Touch of Magic

When witchcraft, voodoo and black magic
are involved, it just might be death
by supernatural causes...

MURDER CHARGES WERE FILED IN MARYLAND on 4 January 2002 against Josephine Gray, 55, dubbed the "Black Widow" for allegedly enticing lovers to kill two husbands and a boyfriend and using voodoo to keep witnesses from testifying against her. "I don't practise voodoo and I don't practise witchcraft," Gray declared when she was charged over her second husband's death. "Just because I go and buy a lucky charm to play the lottery or something or buy herbs and drink herb tea or take olive oil and anoint myself, that's in the Bible."

Gray, who lived in the Maryland suburbs of Washington, scrubbed lavatories and mopped gym floors for most of her adult life, working from 1967 to 1998 as a custodian for the Montgomery County public schools. However, she was described as flamboyant, and fond of heavy makeup and tight skirts. She married Norman Stribbling in 1967, and had five children by him. He was shot dead in his parked car on 4 March 1974. She later collected $16,000 from his life insurance policy.

One relative recently recalled a "magic spell" that she believes led Norman Stribbling uncontrollably to scratch his face to shreds. Two brothers, Donald and Clement Mills, gave statements that they were approached individually by Josephine Gray and her boyfriend, Robert Gray, and offered money to kill Stribbling. The widow and Robert Gray were charged with conspiracy to commit murder, but the charges were dropped after the witnesses disappeared.

According to Robert Gray's family, before he and Josephine met at a part-time job cleaning offices, he was a good husband and a proud father of six children, but after that his whole personality changed. According to his wife Frances, when he stopped eating food cooked by Josephine, he was back to his old self – proof, she said, of her suspicions of witchcraft.

Josephine and Robert had a child and married in 1975. She lost interest in him in October 1990 and threatened his life. He moved out and rented an apartment in Germantown, but was shot dead on 9 November 1990, shortly after an accidental death policy was issued in his name.

Police charged Josephine and her teenage cousin Clarance Goode with murder, but again the charges were dropped because once Josephine was let out on bail, key witnesses changed their stories. Gray received $50,000 in insurance proceeds from her husband's death.

At some point, Gray and her cousin began an affair. By 1996, Goode had decided his life was in danger, according to family members. Goode's body was found in the boot of a car in Baltimore on 21 June 1996, dead from a 9mm gunshot wound, two months after a $100,000 life insurance policy that named Gray as the beneficiary took effect. Goode's sister remembers finding a black voodoo doll with real hair among his possessions. She quickly threw it away. Court documents describe an incantation caught on tape and "voodoo ritual materials" recovered from Gray's home in December 2001.

Stymied for 27 years, police and prosecutors then devised a new strategy, employing a tool frequently used in racketeering cases. In November 2001, a federal grand jury handed up an indictment charging Gray with mail and wire fraud for collecting on the three men's insurance policies. The policies were covered by Maryland's so-called slayer's rule, which prohibits any person who intentionally kills the insured from receiving benefits. Gray's current live-in boyfriend, Andre Savoy, 48, was expected to testify against her, as she was now safely (?) behind bars. *Washington Post, 2 Jan; Independent, 3 Jan; [AP] 5 Jan 2002.*

JOHN OGUNLEYE WAS A 29-YEAR-OLD mechanical engineer in Derby and was born in London of Nigerian parents. In April 1998, he visited his girlfriend Emma Heeks, a teacher at Cheltenham Ladies' College. He went to bed complaining of feeling ill and told her he felt someone "walking over his grave". She found him dead in bed the next morning.

He had appeared to be fit and healthy and doctors could find no reason for his death. Baffled, they called in Home Office pathologist

Stephen Leadbetter. Further investigations by bacteriologists and biologists provided no clues.

At the inquest in Tewkesbury, Gloucestershire, Dr Leadbetter said it was possible that Mr Ogunleye suffered from a "voodoo malaise", in which the victim is made to feel that there is nothing left for them to live for. The coroner recorded a verdict of death due to unascertained natural causes. *D.Mail, 11 Dec 1998.*

ADAM GOTZ, 34, A STUDENT OF ANCIENT Egyptian history from Baden Württemberg, threw himself to his death off the 613ft (187m) Cairo Tower on 28 July 1998 to demonstrate to his friend, Sarah Kilmer, his Pharaonic belief that the dead return to life. He was a "spiritual psychiatrist" who believed the Giza pyramids provided spiritual energy to enable believers to transcend humanity. *[R,AP] 31 July 1998.*

MAGICAL SPIRITS WERE BLAMED for the death of a Melbourne musician and his doctor girlfriend, both of Vietnamese origin, who drowned together in a shallow lagoon on the Pacific island of Erakor in Vanuatu. Mr Vuong Son Ngoc, 36, and Ms Truong Canh Hoang Dieu, 29, were seen on a palm-lined beach at 11.55am on 22 January 2000; 15 minutes later, their bodies were found by a ferryman. Locals said the magic spirit of a sea snake, which had taken others to their deaths, lurked in the crystal-clear waters. "The spirit doesn't like much noise or people picking up shells or starfish," said a tourist guide. A medical examination showed that the couple had drowned, but investigators were at a loss to explain the accident in seemingly peaceful waters, which were only 3ft (1m) deep. *Melbourne Herald Sun, 26 Jan 2000.*

RICARDO YAN, 27, A FILIPINO ACTOR who played romantic heroes, died in his sleep on 29 March 2002, sparking fears that he had been struck down by the 'Sudden Unexplained Nocturnal Death Syndrome" (SUNDS), known in the Philippines as *bangungot*. Victims, nearly always healthy Asian men aged between 30 and 40, are heard moaning just before they die, as if suffering from some form of agony in a terrible nightmare, usually about three o'clock in the morning.

Cardiologist Erdie Fadreguilan of the state-run Philippine General Hospital cited results of autopsies of 328 *bangungot* cases in the Philippines from 1957 to 1987. "We had no way of knowing what happened because they did not survive," he said. The medical diagnosis of Yan's demise was hæmorrhagic pancreatitis leading to cardiac arrest, but this failed to explain why a perfectly healthy young man should be struck down so unexpectedly. Prior to his death, he had drunk the equivalent of two beers, and there was no evidence he had taken any drugs. *[R] 2 April 2002.*

IN SEPTEMBER 2002, WILLIAM POTOGI, 33, WAS GIVEN A ritual bath by a witch doctor in Paramaribo, Surinam, to make him bullet-proof. He asked the witch doctor's assistant to test whether it had worked and was shot dead with his own sawn-off shotgun at point-blank range. According to Ronal Gayadhar, a policeman: "Both men deny murder and claim Potogi died because he lacked faith in the spell".

Ashi Terfa, a traditional healer in Benue state, Nigeria, died in January 2004 after his anti-bullet charm failed a potency test. The herbalist reportedly tied the charm round his neck and asked his client, Umaa Akor, to shoot him. His skull was shattered and Akor was charged with homicide. *[AFP] 5 Sept; Sun, 10 Sept 2002; BBC News, 8 Jan 2004.*

BABA JALLOW, 28, ACCUSED OF STEALING a man's penis through sorcery, was beaten to death on 9 October 2003 by about 10 people in the town of Serekunda in the Gambia, nine miles (14km) from the capital Banjul. For many years, there have been regular reports of penis-snatching in West Africa. Purported victims often claimed that alleged sorcerers simply touched them to make their genitals shrink or disappear in order to extort cash in the promise of a cure – though sometimes the attacker just vanished. *[R] 12 Oct 2003.*

A MAN ACCUSED OF KILLING HIS BROTHER with an axe in the village of Isseluku, southern Nigeria, on 11 September 2006 told police investigators he actually attacked a goat, which was only later magically transformed into his sibling's corpse. "He said that the goats were on his farm and he tried to chase them away," said Police Commissoner Udom Ekpoudom. "When one wouldn't move, he attacked it with an axe. He said it then turned into his brother." *[AP] 15 Sept 2006.*

AN INDIAN MYSTIC ALLEGEDLY KIDNAPPED, beheaded and drank the blood of a toddler in a bid to obtain supernatural powers. Abdul Gafoor, 31, told police he was instructed to do this in a dream. In July 2010 he abducted the 18-month-old boy from a Sufi shrine, where the child's widowed mother was staying in Madurai, an ancient city near the southern tip of the Indian subcontinent. Gafoor and his female associate, Ramala Beevi, 28, then took the child to a lodge in a nearby city, where Gafoor cut his throat. *MX News (Sydney), 26 July 2010.*

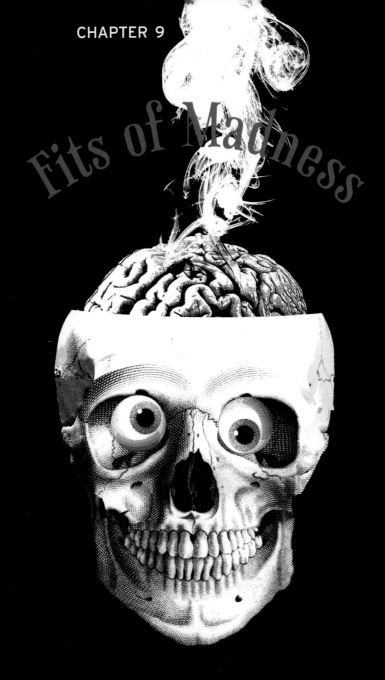

CHAPTER 9

Fits of Madness

Murder, suicide and accidental death can often be
the tragic result of temporary insanity, strange
obsessions or crazy delusions...

IN EARLY NOVEMBER 2001, TAKAKO KONISHI, 28, left her home in Tokyo to travel to North Dakota to hunt for a briefcase containing almost $1 million buried by a fictional character in the 1995 cult film *Fargo*. In the film, a villain played by Steve Buscemi stops his car in a snowy landscape with no features except a wire fence and fence posts, where he buried the case.

On 10 November, Konishi was reported to police in the small city of Bismarck after she was seen wandering near the city dump and Oasis truckstop. When officers interviewed her, she showed them a crude map of a tree next to a highway, supposedly indicating where the money was hidden. "We tried to explain to her that it was a fictional movie and there really wasn't any treasure," said Lt Nick Sevart, but Konishi spoke little English and the police department had no Japanese interpreter. They believe she may have been confused by opening credits for the film, which claimed it was based on a real incident in 1987 – but this wasn't true.

Since she hadn't broken any law, the police had no reason to hold her. They took her to the bus station, where she bought a ticket for Fargo. Two days later, she took a taxi to the village of Detroit Lakes, saying she was interested in seeing the Leonid meteor showers away from city lights. On 15 December, a hunter found her body in woodland near Detroit Lakes, which lies on a road between Fargo and Brainerd. Police, who were waiting for the results of an autopsy, said she was wearing only light clothing and the temperature had dropped to -3°C (26°F) two nights before her body was found. *Bismarck Tribune, 4 Dec; Bergen Record (Hackensack, NJ), 8 Dec; D.Telegraph, 11 Dec 2001.*

SADEQUE ZAMAN, 29, FATALLY STABBED his mother Quamrun Nessa, 53, at their home in Broadlove Lane, Stepney, east London, in December 2003. According to testimony at his Old Bailey trial in August 2004, Zaman had become convinced the deceased had killed his real mother and taken her place – a delusion known as Capgras Syndrome. The key symptom is prosopagnosia, an inability to recognise the facial features of a near-relative. *Shropshire Star, 17 Aug 2004.*

THE BIZARRE SUICIDE OF A QUIET POLITICIAN led officials to warn of a parasitic infection that can make people perform crazy acts. Kevin Keogh, a council chief in Phoenix, Arizona, climbed out of his car at 50mph (80km/h) and leapt to his death on a crowded city street. Doctors believe that he had picked up a rare parasite called cystercosis on holiday in Mexico. It can infect the brain and cause disinhibition. *Times, 18 Dec 2004.*

A MAN TRYING TO WRITE A NOVEL WHILE living in a remote farmhouse led to a scenario reminiscent of Stephen King's memorable horror novel, *The Shining*. John Latham, 29, a diagnosed schizophrenic, was writing the book at Troedyrhiw Farm in the hills behind Port Talbot in South Wales, which his parents, Fay and Joseph, had bought 10 years earlier for the "good life" in the countryside. When his parents looked at his work in February 2004, they found the pages full of "gobbledygook", and shortly afterwards he sprayed himself, the hall and stairs with petrol, causing a fire that killed his father, his 32-year-old brother and himself. Mrs Latham, 54, managed to escape the blaze by jumping out of a window. *Metro, 10 Dec 2004.*

JULES LOWE, 32, WHO ADMITTED BEATING HIS father to death but claimed to have no memory of it, was cleared of murder on 18 March 2005. Edward Lowe, 83, was killed in a prolonged attack at the family home in Walkden, Greater Manchester, in October

2003 after a heavy drinking session. His son then made an "inefficient clean-up" and went to bed. A neighbour called police after seeing the body lying in the drive the next morning. The victim had 90 injuries to his body and had been punched, beaten with a chair and stamped on.

When Lowe told his defence lawyers that he had a history of sleep-walking, he was subjected to "the most detailed scientific tests in British legal history" at Broadmoor in a bid to recreate his reactions on the night of the killing. After hearing expert evidence, the jury at Manchester Crown Court decided that Lowe was sleepwalking in an "automaton" state and was completely unaware of his own actions. The judge ordered Lowe to be remanded in a hospital wing of Strangeways prison until treatment could be arranged at a psychiatric hospital.

The defence of automatism has rarely been employed in the British legal system and was described in court as a "quagmire of law". The day before the Lowe verdict, however, pub landlord Matthew Sadler of Basingstoke, Hampshire, escaped a drink-driving conviction (he was three times over the limit) because the court was persuaded he was sleep-walking – or rather sleepdriving. *Sun, 18 Mar; Guardian, D.Mirror, 19 Mar 2005.*

AN ARTIST WHO DIED IN MARCH 2002 after handcuffing himself to a tree and throwing away the key may have changed his mind and tried to free himself, an inquest heard on 21 September 2005. "There were deep scuff marks on the tree and the cuff was quite high up on his hand instead of on his wrist," said pathologist Brian Rogers. "He could have been there for a few days." The manacled skeleton of Richard Sumner, 47, was found in a remote area of Clocaenog Forest, Denbighshire, by a woman who had become lost while walking her dog in April 2005. He had been dead for three years. The key to the cuffs was found about a metre away from his body.

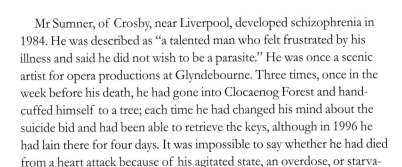

Mr Sumner, of Crosby, near Liverpool, developed schizophrenia in 1984. He was described as "a talented man who felt frustrated by his illness and said he did not wish to be a parasite." He was once a scenic artist for opera productions at Glyndebourne. Three times, once in the week before his death, he had gone into Clocaenog Forest and hand-cuffed himself to a tree; each time he had changed his mind about the suicide bid and had been able to retrieve the keys, although in 1996 he had lain there for four days. It was impossible to say whether he had died from a heart attack because of his agitated state, an overdose, or starvation. The coroner recorded an open verdict. *Western Mail, 21 Sept; BBC News, Metro, 22 Sept 2005.*

KEVIN KIRKLAND, 44, FROM NEWPORT, Shropshire, died on 30 December 2009 after tying himself naked to a tree. He was found with a rope around his penis and wrists. An inquest in Telford was told the computer engineer had injured his wrists in a desperate attempt to free himself. Death was caused by hypothermia and blood loss. *Sun, 10 Aug 2010.*

A MILLIONAIRE INSURANCE EXECUTIVE KILLED his two-year-old daughter after becoming obsessed with *Bug*, a horror film by William 'Exorcist' Friedkin, in which a man and his girlfriend are driven mad by bugs under their skin (a symptom of illusory parasitosis). Spanish-born Alberto Izaga, 36, head of life and health products for Swiss Re, the insurance giant, was a devoted and loving father. On 3 June 2007, he awoke at 4.30am and began talking incoherently to his wife Ligia about the Jesuits and a sect recruiting his fellow executives to take over the financial world, repeated the word "bug" many times and said he hadn't slept for three days. After he had ranted for two hours – "God doesn't exist! The Universe doesn't exist! Humanity doesn't exist!" – his daughter Yanire woke up.

His wife heard him say. "Death! Death! I know what I have to do. I have to kill her! She doesn't exist! Die, die, die! There is nothing left! I have to kill you!" With that he grabbed his daughter and smashed her repeatedly to the wooden floor, believing she had been taken over by a "malign and satanic entity". The little girl suffered multiple skull fractures and brain damage, and was declared dead two days later. The attack took place at the million-pound flat the family lived in on the Albert Embankment overlooking the Houses of Parliament. Izaga was found not guilty of murder by reason of insanity. *Times, D.Mail, Irish Independent, D.Mirror, 12 Jan 2008.*

CHAPTER 10

Killer Critters

Delinquent bears, psychotic seagulls and
flesh-eating pigs are just some of the more
dangerous members of the animal kingdom...

A FRENCH ZOO DIRECTOR WAS CRUSHED to death on 1 November 1999 by a hippopotamus in rut. Jean Ducuing was cycling round the park in Pessac, near Bordeaux, when Komir, a seven-year-old male hippo, charged through an electrified fence after an employee driving a tractor stopped to distribute food. M. Ducuing, aged in his 60s, had trained Komir. Posters for the zoo featured a picture of Komir with M Ducuing's head in his mouth. *[AFP] 2 Nov; Int. Herald Tribune, 3 Nov 1999.*

THREE MOTORISTS WERE KILLED AND dozens more injured by rockslides on the road between the Russian resort cities of Adler and Krasnaya Polyana. People in the area blamed malicious Caucasian bears, which started killing cattle by rolling rocks down the mountains and subsequently graduated to human beings. Not for eating though; Vladimir Tkach, a hunter, said that the creatures were attacking people on the road "just for entertainment". *Independent on Sunday, 20 Oct 2002.*

WHEN A BAT FLEW INTO A HOUSE IN East Mead Township, Pennsylvania, at 1am on 27 May, DJ Delancey tried to whack it with a 3lb (1.3kg) sledgehammer. As he swung the hammer around, he landed a blow on the head of his father-in-law, Francis V Mercier, 66, who was standing behind him. The blow was fatal. *[AP] 28 May 2005.*

A FARMER'S WIFE WAS EATEN ALIVE BY FOUR pigs after falling into their sty. Irma Molnar, 56, who was knocked unconscious, was found clinging to life by her husband Sandor, but she died later in hospital. "Her ears and half her face were missing," said

Dr Dan Grigorescu, of Brasov, Romania. "Her fingers had been bitten off." Sandor vowed to destroy the pigs. *Sun, 5 Mar 2004.*

A YOUNG BOY WAS EATEN ALIVE BY PIGS near his home on the outskirts of New Delhi in India. Three-year-old Ajay was wandering outside with a piece of bread when the pigs attacked him. "We were all having lunch inside the house and didn't realise he had walked out," said Lal Bahadur, the boy's uncle. "A few minutes later, his mother noticed a few pigs chewing something. She began screaming and throwing stones at the pigs after recognising her son's clothes." Only the boy's limbs were recovered. Police arrested the owner of the pigs for causing death by negligence. *Metro, 30 Nov 2006.*

MICHAEL NIKONOV WAS CLAWED AND pecked to death by seagulls when he swam too near their nests on an island in the River Shuya at Petrozavodsk, northwest Russia. He was dead when rescuers reached him. A rescue spokesman said: "He fought hard, but dived down to hide from the gulls and was unable to return to the surface." *Sun, 15 July 2006.*

A BEAR KILLED TWO MILITANTS AFTER discovering them in its den in Indian-administered Kashmir. Two other militants escaped, one of them badly wounded, after the attack in Kulgam district, south of Srinagar. The militants – Mohammad Amin, alias Qaiser, and Bashir Ahmed, known as Saifullah – had Kalashnikov assault rifles but were taken by surprise. Police found the remains of pudding they had made to eat in the cave when the bear attacked. It is thought to be the first such incident since Muslim separatists took up arms against Indian rule in 1989, 20 years earlier. Wildlife experts said the conflict in Kashmir had actually resulted in an increase in the population of bears and leopards. Following the outbreak of the insurgency, people had to hand in their weapons to police – which put a halt to poaching. *BBC News, 3 Nov 2009.*

TAYLOR MITCHELL, 19, A PROMISING FOLK singer from Toronto, was fatally attacked by two coyotes as she hiked alone in Cape Breton National Park, Nova Scotia, on 27 October 2009. Walkers alerted park rangers after hearing her screams. The rangers fired on the coyotes; one escaped unharmed, while the other disappeared in the wilderness after apparently being shot in the leg. Attacks by coyotes on humans are rare; they usually prey on deer and hares. Bleeding heavily from multiple bite wounds, Ms Mitchell was airlifted to hospital, but died of her injuries the following day. *BBC News, 29 Oct; Independent, 30 Oct 2009.*

A WILD BOAR TURNED ON THE HUNTER WHO had shot it and bit the man to death. The man, aged 72, was hunting in Linthe, south of Berlin. He approached the boar, believing he had shot it dead, when it leapt up and attacked. Its teeth punctured a major artery in his leg, causing massive blood loss. Boar had been breeding rapidly in the area, destroying crops, killing pets and attacking people. *Independent, 11 Oct 2008.*

IN AUGUST AND SEPTEMBER 2010, 3,500 people in Peru were bitten by vampire bats, 20 of whom (including five children aged between five and 10) died from rabies. The dead were all members of the indigenous Awajun and Wampis communities, living in the remote north-eastern Peruvian Amazon, close to the border with

Ecuador. Vampire bats usually feed on wildlife or livestock, but are sometimes known to turn to humans for food, particularly in areas where their rainforest habitat has been destroyed. Some local people suggested this latest outbreak of attacks might be linked to the unusually low temperatures in the Peruvian Amazon in recent years. *(London) Eve. Standard, 13 Aug; BBC News, 23 Sept 2010.*

A 20-YEAR-OLD YEMENI BRIDE was killed by a scorpion which a jealous older wife had hidden in the younger woman's wig. Reports from Taiz in south Yemen said the creature was hidden in the hairpiece with the help of a hairdresser. The bride had felt the stings as she was dressed to be taken to her future husband's house, but the coiffeur told her the pain was coming from hairpins. Doctors said she died of 24 stings. Far less poison was enough to be fatal. Muslim men are traditionally allowed up to four wives. *[DPA] Melbourne Herald Sun, 13 Oct 2000.*

A BOLIVIAN FARM WORKER FELL ASLEEP under an ant-infested tree and was killed by insect bites. Beni city police chief Rolando Ramos said Santiago Ortiz, 42, apparently had been drinking before sitting down beneath a Palo Santo tree, known for hosting a particularly aggressive sort of ant. When police reached the scene, Ortiz was dead, with swarms of ants still running across him. *Boston (MA) Herald, 22 July 2009.*

KATIE DAGLEY, 19, WAS KILLED BY A SLUG or snail. She was driving home from work on 4 August 2010 when her Ford Ka collided with a Fiat on a single-lane bridge at Alvecote, near Tamworth, West Midlands. She died at the scene. An investigation

found that traffic lights controlling access to the bridge had malfunctioned 20 minutes before the crash when a slug or snail left a trail of slime across a circuit board. This caused a short-circuit and jammed the lights on green at both ends of the bridge. *D.Mail, Sun, 31 Jan 2011.*

FARMER MARK EVISON, 47, ACCIDENTALLY disturbed a wasps' next while cutting grass for a neighbour in Ellerker, East Yorkshire, on 16 August 2009, and was repeatedly stung on head, neck, and chest. He staggered home and telephoned his brother Paul. "The wasps have got me," he said. Paramedics arrived after 10 minutes and gave him a shot of adrenaline, but it was too late. He died at the scene, less than an hour after being stung. Four days later, Joan Russell, 81, died after being stung on her hand by a wasp in Holt, Norfolk, while doing the washing-up. An average of four people a year die in Britain from wasp, hornet and bee stings. *D.Mirror, D.Mail, 22 Aug 2009.*

A POACHER SETTING ILLEGAL SNARES IN South Africa's vast Kruger National Park was chased off by hippos, and then eaten by lions. Rangers alerted by two other men who fled found part of a skull and ripped clothing two days later. "It appears the dead man was charged and injured by hippos," said an official. "It's impossible to say whether he was alive or dead by the time the lions got to him." *D.Mirror, 25 Mar 2010.*

CHAPTER 11

The Final Straw

You can only push people so far before they finally
snap and something as trivial as a badly-made cup
of tea leads to rage and murder...

A MAN BLED TO DEATH in New Delhi in 1999 after his wife stabbed him for demanding a second cup of tea that she was not ready to serve. Later that year, Abdel-Nasser Nuredeen from the Cairo working class district of Imbaba lost his temper with his wife, Zeinab, when she refused to make him a cup of tea because she was too busy watching the solar eclipse of 11 August. He strangled her in the ensuing quarrel. When he discovered that his wife was limp and lifeless, he carried her to a nearby heart institute, but doctors told him she was dead. *[AFP] 17 Feb; [R] 13 Aug 1999.*

AN EGYPTIAN IN HIS 80s WHO MURDERED his wife after she refused to add an extra spoonful of sugar to his tea was jailed for life in the Nile city of Qena in January 2006. Hassan Ahmed Mohammed electrocuted Ansaf Amin Yusef and chopped up her body when their 40 years of matrimony turned sour. *Gold Coast Bulletin (Quensland), 25 Jan 2006.*

A MAN OF 84 CONFESSED TO KILLING HIS wife because she made him a "disgusting" cup of coffee. He smashed the cup on the floor after taking a few sips, then hit his wife with a hammer. The 72-year-old woman's body was found by a neighbour in Bari, Italy. *Metro, 16 Oct 2001.*

FRANCIS BUHAGIAR, 68, didn't like the breakfast his 76-year-old sister Maria gave him one morning in February 1999 – so he shot her dead, a court in Malta heard. The row is believed to have been over burnt toast. *[R] 3 Mar 1999.*

PAOLO FASANO, 71, from Alessandria in northern Italy, killed his 74-year-old wife Piera for having the television volume turned up too loud as she watched a music festival in February 1999. He hit her with the iron from the ironing board and then strangled her with a tie from the wardrobe. "Then I didn't know what to do," he said, "so I sat down next to her in front of the television. But I lowered the volume." *D.Telegraph, 2 Mar 1999.*

A 42-YEAR-OLD BUSINESSMAN was clubbed to death with a beer bottle in August 1999 when he refused to stop using his mobile phone – which played an irritating melody – in a Hamburg beer garden. He received three calls and also used the phone to contact friends, angering other customers who had complained about the ringing. He was dead by the time an ambulance arrived. The attacker turned himself in a few hours later. The German press claimed it was the first example in Germany of "mobile phone rage". *D.Telegraph, 10 Aug 1999.*

FILIPINO LABOURER RANDY CRUZ killed his neighbour Rogelio Lopez over who had the more famous surname. A witness told police he saw the two men arguing about their surnames as they walked down a Manila street. At the height of the argument, Cruz, 27, repeatedly stabbed Lopez with a knife. *D.Star, 15 Sept 2002.*

A MINNESOTA MAN STABBED AND SHOT his aunt to death after they argued over the flavour of her home-made chilli. Richard Bruestle, 38, of St Paul, was arrested for the murder of Lorene Nell McIntyre, 50. *NY Post, 11 Dec 2002.*

A MAN SHOT HIS BROTHER DEAD AFTER an argument over a television remote control in Spain's south-west Huelva province. Ignacio Ruiz, 34, used a hunting rifle to blow out the television set before shooting Rafael, 39, in the chest. *Independent, 11 Sept 2002.*

WHEN NORMAN STEPHENSON, 56, criticised his lodger, Michael Holleran, 41, for not lifting the lavatory seat when he urinated, Holleran killed him with a sledgehammer. The attack took place in Wealdstone, north London, in August 1999, and Holleran was jailed for life the following March. *Guardian, 25 Mar 2000.*

STEVEN BRASHER, 42, FROM TEXAS, SHOT and killed his long-time friend Willie Lawson, 39, on 5 November 2001 after accusing him of drinking the last beer in his fridge. "There was only two beers left," he said, "so I took one, and I told Willie not to take my last beer." *Newark (NJ) Star Ledger, 6 Dec 2002.*

FERGUS GLEN, 36, FROM WAINUIOMATA in New Zealand, hacked his brother Craig, 33, to death with an axe on 7 March 2002 because he had not been thanked for cooking dinner. "I'm not proud," he said at his trial last November, "but I did it." *Guardian, 12 Nov 2003.*

JOHN ANDREWS, 66, A FARMER FROM MALTON, North Yorkshire, beat his wife Ingaborg, 61, to death after she fed him nothing but jam sandwiches for a month. He was desperate for a hot meal and begged her to make something different. He flipped when he got home from work and found banana sandwiches on the table.

Ingaborg suffered 13 broken ribs. "A working man cannot live on sandwiches," said Mr Andrews, who was jailed for life. *Sun, 26 July 2004.*

WHEN FRANKLIN PAUL CROW, 56, AND Kenneth Matthews, 58, found there was no lavatory paper in the house they shared in Moss Bluff, Florida, on 18 February 2006, they began to argue. Matthews pulled out a rifle, whereupon Crow fatally attacked him with a sledgehammer and a claw hammer. Matthews was beaten so badly he had to be identified by his fingerprints. *[AP] 21 Feb 2006.*

A FOOTBALL-MAD UKRAINIAN FACED murder charges after strangling his wife because she disturbed him while he was watching his home team playing a match on TV. Andriy Voronin, 34, from Kharkov, throttled his wife Gaby, 32, after she continued to ask him questions. A police spokesman said: "He told us he felt he had no other way to shut her up." *(Dublin) Metro, 9 June 2006.*

NOEL QUINTANILLA-VAQUERO, 21, AND William Antonio Serrano, 23, shared an apartment in Houston, Texas. In October 2007, the younger man complained that Serrano's feet had a foul odour, whereupon Serrano grabbed a knife and stabbed his flatmate to death. In July he was sentenced to 35 years in prison. It was claimed that the men had been drinking. *(London) Eve. Standard, 9 July 2008.*

AFTER ALEXANDER ALEXANDROV'S NEIGHBOUR had played the Robbie Williams hit *Angels* non-stop at full volume for a week, Alexandrov finally snapped and strangled him. The 45-year-old, from Pernik in Bulgaria, was jailed for 16 years. *D.Mirror, 23 Dec 2009.*

A CHINESE STUDENT WHO STABBED HIS roommate to death because of his loud snoring was given a suspended death sentence. Guo Liwei, 24, stabbed Zhao Yan, 23, in the chest and back in their room at Jilin Agricultural University in northeast China. Guo previously complained to Zhao and posted a video of him snoring on a university website. *[AP] 27 Mar 2010.*

AFTER AN EVENING'S BAR-HOPPING IN Fort Worth, Texas, a dispute between four men over whether they were going to heaven or hell led to the death of one of them. Clayton Frank Stoker, 21, put a loaded shotgun in his mouth. When Johnny Joslin, 20, tried to take it away, saying, "If you have to shoot somebody, shoot me," the gun went off and fatally wounded Mr Joslin in the chest. Stoker, a Johnson County corrections officer, was subsequently charged with murder. *[R] 30 July; Guardian, 6 Aug 2002.*

A GLOOMY ANGLER STABBED HIS BEST FRIEND to death for being too happy after a drink and drugs binge. Craig Walter, 34, knifed 48-year-old Maurice Wilson 17 times after he said: "I love life". The pair had smoked 15 joints by a canal in east London before the row. Walter, of the Isle of Dogs, was jailed for life. *Sun, 17 Sept 2005.*

CHAPTER 12

Mysteries

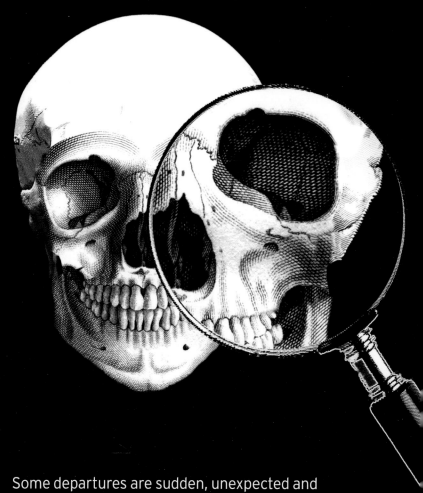

Some departures are sudden, unexpected and utterly inexplicable, baffling the police and leaving investigators scratching their heads...

❓ ANDY CONNELL (38), A FATHER of four, and his friend Kenneth Knapp (23) were found dead at 11am on 19 May 1999 in Connell's Dunlop Tower council flat in the centre of East Kilbride, south of Glasgow. Connell's sister Nancy found them sitting in armchairs, and thought at first they were asleep. The television in front of them was flickering, a video was in the recorder, their heads were propped up against cushions and their legs spread out in front of them. Both had been dead for more than 24 hours.

There was no sign of a forced entry and no injuries on the bodies. The flat had no gas supply, so it wasn't carbon monoxide poisoning; and the post mortem ruled out a drugs link. Knapp had worked in a local pub for a while and Connell was a customer. There was no suggestion that the friendship was in any way unusual. Six weeks later, the deaths remained unexplained. *Sunday Post, 27 June; Scotland on Sunday, 4 July 1999.*

❓ BRYAN SMITH, 43, THE DRIVER whose van nearly killed the horror writer Stephen King in June 1999, was found dead with no sign of injury in his mobile home in Freyeburg, Maine, on 22 September 2000, King's 53rd birthday. He had become increasingly isolated after the accident near North Lovell, Maine, in which King suffered multiple injuries and nearly lost a leg. The sheriff's deputy who discovered the dead man was the officer who had been first on the scene of the road accident. Both Smith and King had Edwin as a middle name. The author of *Carrie* and *The Shining* bought Smith's van for $1,500 and had it crushed in a wrecker's yard. He had pushed for Smith to be charged with assault and mocked him in a *New Yorker* article as "a character out of one of my novels". Smith had received a suspended sentence and lost his driving licence. An autopsy failed to find the cause of death. Toxicology tests would take several months. *[AP] Mirror, 26 Sept; D.Telegraph, Int. Herald Tribune, 27 Sept; Sunday Mail (Queensland), 15 Oct 2000.*

? THE BODY OF DEREK CARMICHAEL, 56, a quality control inspector from Bristol, was found face down in a field of horses in the village of Hallen near Bristol on 13 June 2003. He was wearing a shirt, jumper, moccasins and socks, but his jeans were lying nearby with his underpants in a pocket. He had superficial injuries to his face, but police found no evidence of foul play. A post-mortem examination revealed he suffered from "extremely severe" coronary disease. A pathologist told the inquest on 16 October that the two horses could have caused the injuries to Carmichael's face: "It is possible that they had come across because he was lying still and had attempted to move him." A policeman said it was not known why he was not wearing trousers, but he must have taken them off himself and then put his shoes and socks back on, because if someone had pulled the trousers off, his shoes would have come off too. Verdict: death by natural causes. *[PA] Guardian, 17 Oct 2003.*

. . . .

? WILLIAM O'BRIEN, 41, DISAPPEARED from his home in Boherascrub, Buttevant, Co. Cork, Ireland, in April 2002. Extensive searches by gardaí and civilians failed to turn up any clues. Then on 18 January 2006, his skull was found in a field at Tullig, near Buttevant. Two days later, a bone was found close to a boundary ditch and a dark object was spotted 60ft (18m) up a giant fir tree nearby. It was the rest of O'Brien's skeleton inside his clothes. It was thought the skull had fallen from the tree some time earlier and had been brought into the open field by a fox or dog. The area where the remains were found was about three miles (4.8km) by road, and about a mile and a half (2.4km) cross country, from where O'Brien was last seen near his home. It had not been included in the original search. In any case, as a garda pointed out, "He was so high up the tree and caught in such dense foliage that it would have been very difficult to see him from ground level." Officers ruled out foul play, but declined to speculate how O'Brien ended up in such an unusual location. *Irish Times, 21+23 Jan 2006.*

? PAUL HYDE, 42, AN UNMARRIED, self-employed builder from Barton-on-Humber, Lincolnshire, drank seven or eight pints of beer during a night out celebrating a friend's wedding. He went home at about 12.30am, not apparently drunk. When his sister and brother-in-law called at his house the following afternoon, they found him dead, standing up, with his chin resting on a wall cabinet in the bathroom. A post mortem revealed "no anatomical cause of death". Pathologist Dr Borg Gretch told the inquest in Scunthorpe in February 2002 that the amount of alcohol in Mr Hyde's body could not have killed him. There were no signs of injury and no traces of drugs. The coroner recorded an open verdict. *Sun, 1 Mar 2002.*

? DEAN WARWICK, 62, DROPPED DEAD ON stage after announcing he would name the Antichrist and reveal details about the murder of Bobby Kennedy. He was addressing an audience of conspiracy theorists at a Probe International UK conference in St Anne's, near Blackpool, in October 2006. A theory that Warwick, of Kelso, was murdered by a whistling assassin using a ray gun was posted on David Icke's website. Witnesses said Warwick had expressed fears of being "bumped off" and had complained of a burning sensation at the side of his head. However, his widow insisted he had died of a heart attack. *Sunday Mail, 29 Oct 2006.*

CHAPTER 13

Look Out Below!

Keep your eyes on the skies! Giant hailstones,
falling flowerpots and even plummeting people
can all lead to a sudden demise...

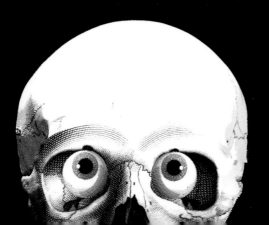

A BELGIAN AIR FORCE PLANE DROPPING crates of food by parachute to starving villagers in the Sudan scored a direct hit on a hut, killing one man and injuring two others. A spokesman for the Belgian Ministry of Defence said: "The hut was hidden by tall grass and the crew didn't spot it until it was too late." *D.Record, 3 Dec 1998.*

ARVIN JAH, 48, WAS KILLED by a plant pot dropped by a monkey from the sixth floor of a block of flats in New Delhi. *Sun, 17 April 2000.*

MARTINIANA ORTIZ WAS KILLED by a bell clapper at about noon on 17 June 2001. The 85-year-old wheelchair-bound woman was sitting in the atrium of San Juanito church in the north-central Mexican city of Aguascalientes during a religious celebration when Uriel Esparza Macias pulled on the bell rope and the 6.5lb (2.9kg) clapper came loose, falling nearly 60ft (18m) onto her head. She was rushed to hospital, but died within two hours. *[AP] San Francisco Chronicle, 19 June 2001.*

HAILSTONES THE SIZE AND SHAPE of eggs – or "as big as *mantou* [wheat flour buns]" – killed 22 (or 25) people and injured 200 when a ferocious storm pummelled the northern parts of Henan province in central China on 19 July 2002. The 25-minute storm caused widespread damage to houses, vehicles, trees and power supplies, particularly in the capital, Zhengzhou, and in Luoyang. Most of the fatalities were caused by buildings collapsing under the weight of the hail, but at least seven resulted from direct hits. Many people were treated for head wounds at local hospitals.

Freak hailstorms have previously hit towns in Nigeria, Australia and Russia, with some reports claiming hailstones the size of footballs. Juan Carlos Oseguera, 19, died when he was hit by "baseball-size" hail in Fort Worth, Texas, sometime around March 2000. Perhaps the largest hailstone on record was one with a circumference of 17in (43cm) that fell on Potter, Nebraska, during a hailstorm on 6 July 1928. *Arizona Republic, ? Mar 2000; [R] 20 July; Mail on Sunday, 21 July; [AFP] New Scientist, Guardian, 22 July 2002.*

AT THE BEGINNING OF APRIL 2007, HAIL "the size of eggs" ravaged five counties in Fujian, on China's south-east coast, killing 13 people, closing a motorway and damaging crops on at least 300 square miles (780 sq km) of farmland. Elsewhere, seven people were killed and one injured when a bus was hit in a landslide triggered by hailstorms in mountainous areas of southwestern Sichuan, and six others were killed by falling roofs and lightning. *[R] 3 April 2007.*

A MAN WAS KILLED BY HAILSTONES IN the southern Spanish province of Jaen. He was working in his garden when he was hit by a sudden storm. "He didn't get a chance to react to the amount of hail that fell in such a short time," said the mayor of the town of Chilluevar. *Bangkok Post, 15 Sept 2007.*

MADDALENA CAMILLO, 72, WAS WALKING in the main square in the village of Sant'Onofrio, in the southern Italian region of Calabria, on 22 September 2004 when a 6ft 6in (2m) metal crucifix fell on her head, killing her. It had been in place for decades, but was dislodged by workers setting up lights for an annual religious festival. *[AP,R] 22 Sept 2004.*

PAOLETTA ORRU, 38, DIED IN FRONT OF HER husband and two children, aged nine and 18 months, when a 3ft (90cm) iron crucifix fell on her. The family was attending a Mass in honour of San Lorenzo, the patron saint of the Sardinian village of Mogorella, near Cagliari. They had been unable to find a place inside the church and were following the service from the steps outside when part of the cornice and the crucifix tore from the façade and hit Mrs Orru, killing her instantly. *(Sydney) D.Telegraph, (Sydney) Morning Herald, D.Record, 12 Aug 2005.*

A DUTCH WOMAN ON HER WAY TO A MEETING about the dangers of objects kept on balconies was killed by a flowerpot that fell from a sixth-floor balcony. The 65-year-old was due to meet a group of fellow residents in Den Bosch, including the owner of the flowerpot. *(London) Evening Standard, 30 Aug 2005.*

BETWEEN 23 FEBRUARY AND 25 February 2008, icicles falling from buildings in the central Russian region of Samara killed six people. Plummeting chunks of ice are an annual hazard for pedestrians in Russia during the spring when the Sun finally melts thick layers of ice and snow that build up on roofs over months of freezing temperatures and darkness. Medical authorities said five people suffered death-by-icicle in the city of Samara and another person in the nearby town of Otradny. *[R] 26 Feb 2008.*

FALLING ICICLES AND ICE BLOCKS KILLED five people and injured 147 in St Petersburg in 2010 following Russia's coldest winter in 30 years. The high toll prompted residents and relatives of victims to demand action against those responsible for what they believe to be careless clearing of ice from rooftops. City Hall said that accidents were inevitable, given the scale of the ice-clearing after such a severe winter. "There are 13,500 roofs in St Petersburg," said Yury Osipov, head of the city's housing committee. "With the current record snowfalls, the roofs should be cleared weekly to prevent blocks of ice forming. That's impossible, not least because it would paralyse traffic in the city." In January 2011, a boy of six was killed by an icicle falling from a five-storey building in St Petersburg. *The Australian, 3 Mar 2008; D.Telegraph, 24 Mar 2010; Sun, 15 Jan 2011.*

A BIBLE WEIGHING ABOUT 3lb (1.4kg) was accidentally knocked off a hotel's 12th-floor balcony in Lins, Brazil. It landed on the head of Charles Maurois, 71, a French tourist sunbathing below, and killed him. Insurers claimed it was an act of God. *Sunday Mail (Scotland), 27 May; Sunday Mercury, 3 June 2001.*

LUDWIK LISZKA, PROFESSOR EMERITUS at the Institute for Space Physics at the University of Umeå in Sweden, says that he knows of only one confirmed case of a person being killed by a falling meteorite. It happened on 20 May 1900 in the village of Kvavisträsk in the Swedish province of Västerbotten. In the evening of that day, villagers were alerted by a horrible roar and a dazzling light when a flaming meteorite fell to the ground. Afterwards they found Ludvig Lundberg, 55, on the road about 50m (160ft) from the impact crater. He had been on his way to visit a neighbour when he was hurled to the ground by the shockwave caused by the impact. Three or four days later, he died in the cottage hospital of internal bleeding. According to Prof Liszka, a meteorite impact of this size would have had an effect similar to a bomb; although Lundberg was not actually hit by the meteorite, he was too close to the point of impact to survive.

The incident is described in a book called *Qvafvisträsk* (which is the old spelling of the name Kvavisträsk), edited by Kjell Johansson, who grew up in this village in the 1930s and 1940s, when there were still many people alive who remembered, and often talked about, Ludvig Lundberg's death in the blast wave of a shooting star. The impact crater, where the "star" hit the ground, is still there for everyone to see, says Johansson. *Sydsvenskan (Sweden), 23 Nov 2008.*

A WIDOW NAMED LAM WAS COLLECTING clothes from a drying rack on the balcony of her 27th-floor apartment in the Ma On Shan district of Hong Kong last March when she slipped and plunged to the ground. She landed on Chan Kwai-mui, 51, a cleaner on her way to work. Both women were killed. A couple of weeks later, another widow, this one suicidal, leapt from a 12th-floor balcony and landed on a stranger, killing both of them. Raymonde Demares, 62, dressed in pyjamas, crushed smartly dressed sports journalist Herman Lingg, 72, as he entered the apartment block in Brussels. She had been depressed since the death of her husband. The same thing happened a third time in northern Chile in May, when Josefina Venizela jumped from the 12th-floor of a building and landed on Luisa Almendares, a 56-year-old cleaning lady, who happened to be taking out the rubbish from the building next door. Both women were killed. *www.weirdasianews.com, 2 Mar; D.Express, 25 Mar; Irish Independent, 29 May 2010.*

CHAPTER 14

The Perils of Karaoke

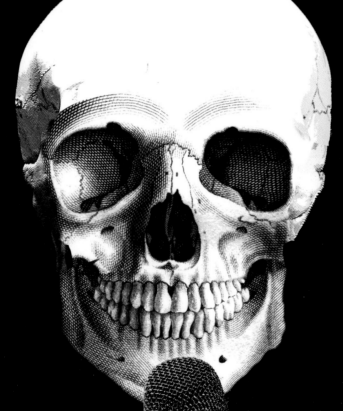

Is it really any surprise that the combination of freely-flowing alcohol and out-of-tune renditions of 'My Way' so often ends in death?

ONE MAN WAS KILLED AND ANOTHER wounded in the Philippines in November 2001 when a fight broke out at a karaoke bar in Manila over the quality of the singing. Many karaoke clubs in the country had already removed Frank Sinatra's *My Way* from their playlists because so many fights broke out as the egocentric anthem was being performed. In July 1998, drunken revellers fatally stabbed Ely Dignadice, 29, after he sang an off-key rendition of a popular love song, *Remember Me*, at a Manila karaoke bar. His performance drew jeers from 10 men, who later attacked him with knives, bottles, wooden clubs and a gun. *Independent, 7 July 1998; Scotsman, 11 July; Sunday Times, 25 Nov 2001.*

WHEN TWO FILIPINO MEN SARCASTICALLY applauded a student's off-key rendition of *My Way* in a Manila karaoke parlour in February 2002, a fight broke out. The two left to avoid further trouble, but the 21-year-old student ambushed and shot them outside. One was killed and the other seriously injured. Casimiro Lagugad, 25, was asked to sing *My Way* during a birthday party in Caloocan, a suburb of Manila, on 22 June 2003. Annoyed that he was singing out of tune, his neighbour Julio Tugas, 48, stabbed him in the neck. Lagugad was rushed to hospital, but died while being treated. Tugas later surrendered to the authorities. "And now the end is near/And so I face the final curtain" all too often comes true. *[R] 19 Feb 2002; [DPA] Sydney Morning Herald, 25 June 2003.*

KARAOKE IS IMMENSELY POPULAR IN THE Philippines; stand-alone karaoke machines can be found in the unlikeliest of settings, including outdoors in rural areas, where men can sometimes be seen singing early in the morning. *My Way* remains one of the most popular song choices in the country, which is home to more than a million illegal guns and has a culture of violence, drinking and machismo. "I used to like *My Way*, but after all the trouble I stopped singing it," said Rodolfo Gregorio, 63, a Filipino barber and keen karaoke singer. "The trouble with *My Way* is that everyone knows it and everyone has an opinion. You can get killed."

In one case, Romy Baligula, 29, was shot dead in the city of San Mateo in 2007. He was halfway through *My Way* when a security guard shouted that he was out of tune. He carried on regardless and the guard shot him in the chest with a revolver. *Int. Herald Tribune, 8 Feb; D.Telegraph, Independent, 10 Feb 2010.*

MY WAY KILLINGS ARE NOT CONFINED to the Philippines. In December 1992, for instance, diners at a sushi bar in Toronto, Canada, watched in disbelief as a furious karaoke performer, who had been crooning a Vietnamese dialect version of *My Way*, flung down his microphone and shot two members of the audience in the head. Tan Ngoc Le, 22, was killed and Khanh Van Cao, 25, was hospitalised. Far from laughing at the performance, they had been smiling their appreciation. "There was nothing wrong with his singing," said Khe Ba Lin, a waiter. "He was actually quite good." *D.Mail, 3 Dec 1992.*

BETWEEN 1989 AND 2001, SIX PEOPLE WERE shot dead in Thailand while fighting over possession of karaoke machines. In a Bangkok karaoke bar in February 1994, Thai property tycoon Chen Ka Sek hogged the microphone for three hours and sang *Candle in the Wind* three times. When another man asked to have a go, Mr Sek had his bodyguards shoot the presumptuous fellow dead. "We were carried away by the beauty of my voice," said Mr Sek.

In 2000, Thai policeman Jirawat Sangworn, 25, shot and killed one man and wounded a friend. He was about to sing the same song for the third time when the pair began heckling. Another victim was village headman Pichet Iamfuang, 37, killed on 9 July 2001. Also in Thailand, some time in 2008, a man shot dead eight of his neighbours after they repeatedly sang John Denver's *Take Me Home, Country Roads. Guardian, 2 Mar; Big Issue, 8-14 Mar 1994; Scotsman, 11 July; Sunday Times, 25 Nov 2001; Guardian, 6 Dec 2008.*

ON 3 DECEMBER 2008, ABDUL SANI DOLI, 23, refused to stop singing and hand over the microphone at a coffee shop that doubled as a karaoke bar in the town of Sandakan, Borneo. Three men on a nearby table confronted him outside the coffee shop, where a heated argument developed and Doli was fatally stabbed in the chest. Two men were arrested on suspicion of murder. *The Star (Malaysia), BBC News, 5 Dec; Guardian, 6 Dec 2008.*

A CATHOLIC PRIEST WAS ELECTROCUTED AT A beach party in the Philippines resort of Morong on 7 April 2008. Father Roberto del Rosario had just emerged from a dip in the sea and was dripping wet when he took the microphone of a karaoke machine. Companions said they saw him trembling as he held the mike. He lost consciousness and was declared dead on arrival in hospital. *MX News (Brisbane), 11 April 2008.*

CHAPTER 15

Ironic Exits

Comedy and tragedy are often two sides of the
same coin where death is concerned, as this
collection of unlikely demises demonstrates...

JOSE RICART, 53, WAS RUN OVER AND KILLED by a truck while crossing the road in Burgos, Spain, while carrying a banner that proclaimed (in Spanish): "The end of the world is nigh" *Sun, 18 Sept 1998.*

EGYPTIAN GOVERNMENT WORKER ADEL Nasim Gerges, 50, who had waited eight years for promotion, died of a heart attack when he saw his name on a notice board listing thousands of promotions. "He fell victim to the dream which had finally come true," as a Cairo newspaper put it. *Wolverhampton Express & Star, Halifax Eve. Courier, 18 Feb 1999.*

KATHLEEN YEOMAN, A 46-YEAR-OLD divorced mother of two, staged an elaborate fake burglary to win back the affection of Paul Cockerill, her neighbour in Brixworth, Northamptonshire, on 30 October 1998. She ransacked her house, tipping out drawers and throwing jewellery on her bed. She piled electrical goods in the front room, taped her mouth, put a plastic bag over her head and tied her hands together.

Leaving her front door open, she lay across the front doorstep of her former lover. As she waited for his return from a pub, she vomited and, unable to remove the tape from her mouth as her hands were shackled with self-tightening plastic ties, she choked to death. Police at first treated the death as suspicious, but they reviewed the case when they found that nothing had been taken and she still had £918 in her handbag. *Times, D.Telegraph, 1 July 1999.*

⚠ **EXIT** HUANG TZU-HENG, 20, WANTED TO TEST HIS girl-friend's love. So the Taipei shop assistant posed as a "Mr J" and emailed her. An online relationship developed even as the girl, Hsiao Ian, continued dating Huang. Hsiao then told Huang that she wanted to break up with him because she had fallen in love with a Mr J. As a result, Huang went home and killed himself, leaving a note explaining that he and Mr J were one and the same. *Independent on Sunday, 27 July 2003.*

⚠ **EXIT** CECIL AND TERI LYNN CARVER (38 AND 35) were in bed in Rose, Oklahoma, on 24 February 2004 when they began arguing about a daytime television show they were watching. He hit her, then fired his gun into the headboard. She phoned police, he tried to stop her, and, in the ensuing melée, was fatally shot. The subject of the television show was how to survive domestic violence. *Gold Coast (Queensland) Weekend Bulletin, Independent on Sunday, 13-14 Mar 2004.*

⚠ **EXIT** CATHERINE OSLIFFE, 34, A LECTURER IN anger management at Garth prison, near Leyland, stabbed her husband Roger, 35, to death a week after they returned from a honeymoon cruise. After he threw a vase and its contents over her head as she lay in bed on 6 June 2004, she went downstairs and armed herself with a kitchen knife. He bled to death in Blackburn Royal Infirmary. She was jailed for five years. *D.Telegraph, 2 Feb 2005.*

⚠ **EXIT** ALISON TAYLOR, 36, LOST HER TEMPER in September 2004 when her Peugeot 405 wouldn't start, so she laid about the engine with a hammer. The blows set off the broken starter motor.

Even though the ignition was switched off, the circuit was still live and the engine started. The car lurched forward because the handbrake was broken. Knocked off-balance, Ms Taylor of Camperdown, North Tyneside, reached out and grabbed the throttle cable, which made the car accelerate over her. The 1.3 tonne vehicle rolled down a grass embankment, fatally crushing her. Ironically, the family had planned to get rid of the car that week. *D.Mirror, 13 April 2005.*

VICTORIA DELECROIX WAS KILLED IN A PLANE taking her to a skydiving jump to conquer her fear of heights. She was one of four people who died when their De Havilland Twin Otter plane suffered engine failure and smashed into an electricity pylon in Sullivan, Missouri, on 29 July 2006. The 22-year-old, from Beckenham in southeast London, a graduate of Derby University, had been in America since June working at a summer camp for the disabled. *Times, (London) Eve. Standard, Metro, 3 Aug 2006.*

A GOOD LUCK TALISMAN WORN BY A Malaysian man brought him the ultimate misfortune when a lightning bolt struck the copper emblem he wore around his waist on 3 June 2009 and killed him instantly. Champee Kelean, 46, died while taking shelter under a shed during a storm in the northern state of Kedah. It was thought his talisman had attracted the bolt of lightning. *Malaysian Star, via Adelaide Advertiser, 6 June 2009.*

DEBORAH PARKER, 61, A WORLD-FAMOUS health expert who campaigned to stop pregnant women from smoking, died of lung cancer – but had never smoked in her life. Her husband Matthew said her death was a "cruel irony". She was professor of public health at Salford University in Greater Manchester. *Sun, 27 Oct 2009.*

TWELVE INDONESIAN CHILDREN DIED ON 6 June while taking part in a ceremony to dispel bad luck after a measles outbreak in a remote village in Aceh province, Sumatra. "There were 37 kids gathered together on a wire-cable suspension bridge when it collapsed and they fell into a river," said district chief Ibnu Hasyim; 25 were rescued with minor injuries, but 12 others, aged 12 and younger, were swept away in the strong currents. The children were watching adults throwing chickens into the river as an offering. *[AFP] 8 June 2010.*

A SUPERSTITIOUS MAN WHO REFUSED TO leave his home on Friday 13th died in his kitchen after he was stung by a rare breed of wasp. Florin Carcu, 54, was making coffee when he was stung at his home in Cluj, central Romania. His boss Gheorghe Domsa said: "He took the day off because he seemed scared of something bad happening." *Metro, some time in 2007.*

A WOMAN IN BRAZIL WAS KILLED BY THE coffin carrying her late husband when the hearse they were travelling in was involved in a crash. Marciana Silva Barcelos, 67, was on the way to the cemetery in Alvorada to bury her husband, Josi Silveira Coimbra, 76, who had died of a heart attack after attending a dance the previous night. The hearse was struck from behind by an Alfa Romeo car and the coffin slammed into the head of the widow, who was sitting in the passenger seat, killing her instantly. The couple's son and the driver of the hearse suffered minor injuries in the accident, about 70 miles (112km) south of Porto Alegre in the state of Rio Grande do Sul. *[R] BBC News, 11 Nov 2008.*

△ GIOVANNI GRECO SENT HIMSELF, LITERALLY, to an
E☠IT early grave. Greco, 63, was so keen that his future mausoleum would be a perfect fit that he liked to visit it to ensure the builders were making it just right. He made his regular trip to the construction site in the small cemetery in his hometown of Lascari, near Palermo in Sicily, on 1 September 2002. He climbed a ladder to get a better view of the top of the mausoleum when he slipped, hit his head on a marble step, and fell into his own tomb.

A year earlier, another Sicilian died after falling into an empty grave in a Palermo cemetery. Marcello Petrola, 31, intended bringing some flowers to the tomb of a dead relative when he was forced to dodge an approaching car. He put his foot on a marble tombstone, which broke in half and dropped him into the 20ft (6m) deep grave, which swallowed him up. *[R] 4 Sept; Guardian, 6 Sept; Gold Coast (Queensland) Weekend Bulletin, 7-8 Sept 2002.*

🛠 A CATHOLIC WHO WENT TO CHURCH TO GIVE thanks
after being rescued from a jammed lift was killed when a stone altar fell on him. Gunther Link, 45, died instantly as he was crushed under the 860lb (390kg) altar in the Weinhaus Church in Vienna, Austria. "He seems to have embraced a stone pillar on which the stone altar was perched and it fell on him," a police spokesman said. *D.Telegraph, Ananova, 11 Sept 2009.*

CHAPTER 16

Fatal Fish

You should never underestimate the denizens of the deep, as these ill-fated fishermen and unfortunate anglers could testify – if they were still alive...

HARRIS SIMBAWA (OR SIMWABA) CAUGHT A fish on the banks of the Chengu River, near Livingstone, Zambia, in October 1998. He tried to bite its head, the local method used to kill fish; but the catch slipped down his throat, choking him to death. Villagers found his body with a stick dangling from his mouth. He had apparently tried to dislodge the fish with the stick, but had only pushed it further down his gullet. *D.Telegraph, Johannesburg Citizen, 28 Oct 1998.*

A SIMILAR FATE MET TODD ANKER LAWER, although the circumstances were more puzzling. The 36-year-old transient was found dead in Salmon Creek Park, Vancouver, Washington State, on 25 July 1998. A bluegill fish, about 5in (13cm) long, was lodged in his throat and an autopsy showed he had died of asphyxiation. He was dressed only in shorts, but his other clothes were found nearby. The shorts were not wet and there was no indication he had been in the water, although one witness saw him sitting near the water. *The Oregonian (Portland, OR), 28 July 1998.*

A 62-YEAR-OLD MAN CHOKED TO death in 2002 after swallowing a live octopus at his home in Seoul, South Korea. Doctors removed the octopus, which was still alive and clinging to the man's gullet. Live octopus is a popular but often fatal Korean snack – choking six people a year. *D. Mirror, 30 April 2002.*

LIM VANTHAN, 17, AND HIS FAMILY WERE planting rice on 16 August 2003 near their home on the outskirts of the Cambodian capital Phnom Penh when they decided to go for a swim. During his dip, Lim caught a prized 8in (20cm) *kantrob* fish with his hands, but it jumped out of his grasp and lodged in his throat, where it became stuck because of barbs running down its back. He died of suffocation before he could receive treatment. *[R] 19 Aug 2003.*

A CHINESE FISHERMAN was killed by a two-foot (60cm) long arrowfish when it leapt from the sea and struck his abdomen, skewering his lungs with its pointed head. The young man, from the south-eastern province of Fujian, was fishing with a lamp from a small boat when the green fish, which has sharp spines and a long, sword-like "beak", shot out of the water. A fishery official said the fish might have been frightened by the lamp. *D.Telegraph, 27 June 2000.*

A MONSTER CATFISH SAID TO be 9ft (2.7m) long pulled an angler into a lake and towed him to his death. Anto Schwarz, 45, shouted to his friends that he had hooked a huge one as his rod bent double. After a struggle lasting several minutes, the fish pulled him off balance and Schwarz, entangled in his line and unable to swim, drowned in Eva Maria Lake near Vienna. The huge fish lurking in Austrian lakes and rivers are legendary. *D.Express, 26 July 2000.*

AN ANGLER DROWNED IN THE THAMES ONE night in August 2003 when a powerful barbel tugged on his line. Stanley King, 60, who was recovering from an operation, was dragged into the water by the 3.5lb (1.6kg) fish. He then became tangled in the line of his second rod and the hook became embedded in his trouser leg. His body was not found until the following morning and his gumboots were recovered separately. Mr King, of Harpenden, Hertfordshire, was at his favourite fishing spot in Windsor, Berkshire, with a friend of 38 years, John Speer, 82, testing new equipment. Mr Speer head a splash and his friend frantically calling "John, John, I've gone in!" Crippled with rheumatoid arthritis and able to move only with crutches, he could do no more than shine his fisherman's lamp through the trees and shout to his friend to swim towards the light. The rod was later found downstream with the fish still attached. *D.Telegraph, Sun, 6 Dec 2003.*

ANOTHER ANGLER WAS KILLED ON 17 August 2003 when he was swept out to sea after hooking a giant conger eel in a competition. Farm labourer Albert Marshall, 43, was standing on an outcrop known as Fox's Snout in Kirkcudbright Bay, Dumfries and Galloway, when he was hit by a freak wave and dragged away. His companion, who was fishing nearby, raised the alarm, but a rescue attempt involving a helicopter and four lifeboats was unsuccessful. Conger eels are notoriously strong and can put up a tremendous fight when hooked. They can grow up to 10ft (3m) long and weigh as much as 250lb (113kg). They also have extremely sharp teeth and strong jaws and are said to eat just about anything that moves. *D.Mail, 18 Aug 2003.*

JUDY ZAGORSKI, 57, OF PIGEON, MICHIGAN, was sunbathing on the bow of a small fishing boat off the city of Marathon in the Florida Keys on 20 March 2008 when a stingray leaped out of the water, knocking her to the deck, where she hit her head. She was taken to hospital in Tavernier, where she was pronounced dead. The impact is likely to have killed both her and the ray. Investigators initially said one of the ray's venomous barbs had stabbed her in the neck, but they later admitted there was no sign of a puncture. The 77lb (35kg) ray had a wingspan of 5-6ft (1.5-1.8m), and the boat had been travelling at about 25mph (40km/h). Rays sometimes jump out of the water when they feel threatened and it has been known for rays to mistake the shadow of a fast-moving boat for that of a shark. Eagle rays, also called leopard rays or bonnet skates, can have a wingspan of up to 10ft (3m), and, with an 8ft (2.4m)-long tail, weigh up to 500lb (227kg). They have between two and six short, venomous barbs near the base of their whip-like tails.

Rays jump to escape a predator, give birth, or shake off parasites, but aren't known for attacking people. However, this wasn't the first such incident in Florida. A spotted eagle ray leapt out of another boat in the Fort Lauderdale area in October 2003 and stung James Bertakis, 81. Although the barb entered his heart chamber, he made an almost complete recovery. Not so lucky was Steve Irwin, the Australian wildlife expert, who died a month earlier when a stingray's barb pierced his heart as he swam near Port Douglas in Queensland. *[R] D.Telegraph, 21 Mar; (Sydney) D.Telegraph, 22 Mar 2008.*

DUONG TRONG ANH, A 16-YEAR-OLD Vietnamese boy, died after being stabbed through the heart by a metre-long needle-fish as he was diving for sea cucumber in Halong Bay, 200km (124 miles) east of Hanoi. Duong's companions saw the fish stuck in his chest and pulled out the needle-like snout, but he died from the wound soon after. His family was considering burying the fish beside him. *[DPA] Bangkok Post, 11 Sept 2007.*

A GIANT CATFISH CALLED A GOONCH was thought responsible for several deaths in the Great Kali, a river flowing along the Indian-Nepali border. Local people believed it had developed a taste for human flesh after feasting on partially burnt corpses from funeral pyres. The mysterious fish, perhaps an oversized mutant, was thought to have taken a 17-year-old Nepali boy in April 1988. Witnesses said he was cooling himself in the river when something pulled him below the surface. Three months later, a small boy was dragged under as his father watched helplessly. And in 2007, an 18-year-old Nepali disappeared in the river, after being dragged down by something described as like an "elongated pig". In 2008, British biologist Jeremy Wade caught a Great Kali goonch that weighed 161lb (73kg) and was nearly 6ft (1.8m) long. "If that got hold of you," he said, "there'd be no getting away." *Sun, 9 Oct; Weekend Australian, 11/12 Oct 2008.*

A 59-YEAR-OLD CHEF DIED AFTER A 50cm (20in) Asian swamp eel was put up his bottom. Doctors in Sichuan, China, found the marine creature in the man's rectum after his death in April 2010. It had allegedly been inserted after the man passed out drunk, by "pals" playing a prank. Doctors said the eel had devoured his bowels. *Sun, 30 April 2010.*

Off with their Heads!

Some are lopped off
by passing loonies,
others removed in DIY
self-decapitations – but
losing your head is never
a nice way to go...

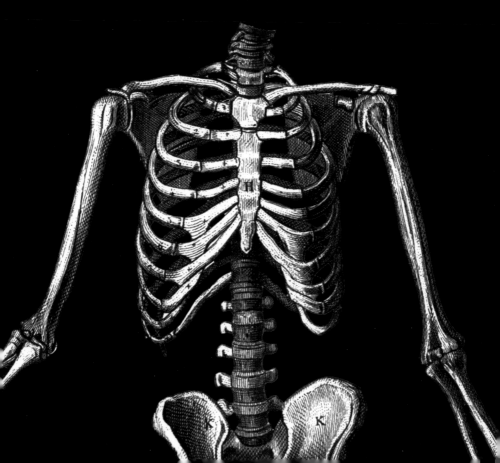

A DRIVER DECAPITATED HIMSELF BY tying a long rope from his neck to a lamppost and accelerating away. A passer-by found his head on the pavement in the Lancashire Hill area of Stockport, Greater Manchester, on 10 October 2001. Police found the headless torso at the wheel of a Citroen Saxo that had crashed through a fence a short distance away. At the time of the report, the man had not been formally identified. *Sun, 11 Oct 2001.*

LEONARD NEWTON, 50, FROM BRISTOL, wrapped his seatbelt round his neck and crashed his car into cliffs at Cheddar Gorge, Somerset, in October 2001, beheading himself. On 16 January 2002, Paul Marston, 33, from Nuneaton, tied one end of a yellow tow-rope round his neck and the other to a lamppost. He then drove off at speed in his silver Cavalier car, decapitating himself. His head was seen lying in the middle of the road by a student who was giving his girlfriend a driving lesson. *Bristol Eve. Post, 1 Mar; Heartland Eve. News, 10 April 2002.*

A DRUNKEN DRIVER RAN OFF THE ROAD on 28 August and sideswiped a telegraph pole support wire, decapitating his best friend, who was hanging out the passenger window feeling nauseous. John Kemper Hutcherson, 21, then drove 12 miles (19km) back to his house in suburban Atlanta, Georgia, and went to sleep in his bloody clothes, leaving the headless body in the truck. A neighbour walking by with his baby daughter the following morning discovered the torso of Francis Daniel Brohm, 23, in the parked truck and called the police. The head was found in the bushes near the pole. It appeared that Hutcherson was unaware of the death until informed by police. *Newsday, 31 Aug 2004.*

A MAN LEFT TRAUMATISED BY THE BOXING DAY tsunami disaster in 2004 decapitated himself in a secluded car park on 6 January 2005. Daniel Watson, 31, tied a rope around his neck and attached the other end to a tree near the grounds of Crystal Palace National Sports Centre in south London. He then drove way and his head was torn from his body. Hearing his blue Metro hurtling down a grass bank and smashing into a tree, Sports Centre staff rushed out and found his headless torso. The dead man was engaged to be married and had returned from a trip to Thailand weeks before the tsunami struck. His family said the shock of watching television pictures of the disaster left him depressed and frustrated. *South London Press, 18 Jan 2005.*

COLIN VINCENT, a 57-year-old handyman, decapitated himself on 13 October 1999, two months to the day after the death of his beloved wife Joan from cancer. He had constructed a guillotine with a drop of 10ft (3m) in the stairwell of an outside cellar at his home in Halifax, West Yorkshire. When police found him, there was a spirit level nearby which he had used to check that the blade was set truly and wouldn't jar. His head had been cleanly decapitated through the lower part of the neck. In his left hand he still had a pair of pliers that he had used to cut the retaining wire and release the extremely heavy blade, which required three men to move. The guillotine had obviously taken quite some time to construct, and was very well constructed. There was evidence to indicate that some test drops had been made. *D.Telegraph, Times, Yorkshire Post, 3 Dec 1999.*

ANOTHER DIY DECAPITATION took place near Virnagar in the western Indian province of Kathiawar at midnight on 18 February 1996, during the festival of Mahashivatri. Lalji Arjanbhai Patel, a 28-year-old man well known in the district as a devotee of Shiva, with a wife, two daughters and a son, decapitated himself after offering prayers at the lonely hilltop temple of Mahadevia dhar. The temple, built in 1875, no longer had a regular priest.

Patel suspended a sickle from the ceiling with rope, and held one end. Bowing before the Shivalingham (Shiva's ritual stone phallus), he released the rope. The sickle fell at the base of his neck, severing it instantly, while his blood flowed into the channels round the lingham as a sacrificial offering. Villagers of the Hanuman Kharachiya village, where Patel tilled a small plot of land, claimed that he had been talking of offering the "formidable *Kamalpuja* of the Shivling" for the previous three days. *Indian Express, 20 Feb 1996.*

A MAN BEHEADED HIMSELF WITH A home-made guillotine he made secretly in his bedroom. The body of Boyd Taylor, 36, was found on 13 January 2003 by his father, with whom he ran a building firm, at the house they shared in Milbourne, near Ponteland, Northumberland. An electrical timer, thought to have been used to activate a heavy blade weighted with paving stones, was attached to the 8ft by 3ft (2.4m by 90cm) machine. The blade came down at 3.30am, as Mr Taylor lay on an airbed beneath the machine, which was modelled on the guillotine used during the French Revolution. *Newcastle Journal, D.Telegraph, D.Mirror, 16 Jan 2003.*

A 56-YEAR-OLD PLUMBER, IDENTIFIED only as Frantisek, was so distraught over his unpaid taxes that he took a home-made guillotine to a tax office in Malacky, western Slovakia, and lopped off his own head. As curious passers-by watched, he put his head in the slot and let the blade fall. The man, from the village of Zohora, owed 25,000 koruna (£640) in taxes and 15,000 koruna (£380) in penalties. *Gold Coast (Queensland) Bulletin, 9 May 2002.*

ON 16 AUGUST 2003, HITOSHI NIKAIDOH, 35, of Dallas, Texas, was decapitated by a malfunctioning elevator at Christus St. Joseph Hospital in Houston where he was a surgical resident. The doors closed on the second floor, pinning his shoulders, and then the elevator car moved upwards, severing his head, which landed in the car beside a female hospital worker. The car then jammed between floors, trapping the hysterical woman with the head for 20 minutes before fire crews could reach her. Japanese-born Dr Nikaidoh had planned to become a Christian missionary. *Houston Chronicle, 17 Aug; [AP] 18 Aug; Sun, 19 Aug 2003.*

A HEADLESS MAN WAS FOUND IN A car park in Darmstadt, Germany, two miles (3.2km) from Castle Frankenstein. The ruined castle was the birthplace in 1673 of Johann Konrad Dippel von Frankenstein, an alchemist famous for his interest in the creation of artificial life. He was rumoured to have experimented with human body parts and may have inspired the character of Victor Frankenstein in Mary Shelley's 1818 novel. Police dismissed suggestions of a link between the castle, a popular tourist attraction with Gothic thrill-seekers, and the decapitated man as "absurd". *USA Today, Toronto National Post, 18 June 2003.*

CROWDS IN A BUSY MARKET FLED IN TERROR as a blood-soaked woman walked among them, holding a man's severed head high like a trophy. This grand guignol scene was played out in October 2008 in the village of Makkapurva, 270km (170 miles) southeast of Lucknow in India. According to police officer Ram Bharose, the unnamed 35-year-old woman had sliced off the man's head with a sickle she had been using to cut grass near her village. "She was getting grass for her cattle when the man came up from behind her and tried to sexually assault her," said Bharose. "In a bid to save her dignity, she turned on him and during a struggle managed to chop off his head with the sickle. We have no doubts about her story because she has bite marks on her neck and cheek." She said her attacker had been stalking her for three months. *MX News (Brisbane), 20 Oct 2008.*

DEBU SAHA, 22, WAS ARRESTED FOR BEHEADING his neighbour, Gobindra Mondal, 80, as he slept in his home north of Kolkata (Calcutta) in India. He told police he had dreamed that the flooding of the Fulahar river could be checked if he made a human sacrifice. (Sydney) *D.Telegraph, 26 July 2004.*

DAVID PHYALL, 58, HAD LIVED IN HIS housing association flat at Bishopstoke in Eastleigh, Hampshire, since 2000 and was fighting to stay there despite plans to bulldoze the entire area and rebuild it. After receiving an eviction notice, he cut off his own head with a chainsaw. He was the last resident on the estate; all 71 surrounding flats were empty. *D.Mail, 14 July 2008.*

A 22-YEAR-OLD MAN BEHEADED THREE people with a spade to "celebrate" Hitler's birthday in Chernigov, Ukraine. *Sun, 23 April 2010.*

CHAPTER 18

Follow the Leader

Sometimes one fatality inevitably leads to others in
a sort of deadly domino effect, and whole families
are taken out when 'the shit hits the clan'...

⫻ SEVEN PEOPLE DIED IN SUCCESSION while trying to rescue each other in southern China on 2 May 2001, according to state-sponsored *Wen Wei Po* daily. Ding Yonghua fell into a well in a village in Baiyun district, Guangzhou. Five of his relatives, including a husband and wife, followed each other into the well, each one going down after the others failed to emerge, "not realising it was filled with odourless and colourless poison". A security guard at nearby roadworks was summoned, but he too succumbed. Villagers called the police, who brought in exhaust fans and oxygen tanks, and pulled out seven bodies. *[AFP] 4 May 2001.*

⫻ MAJID LANAPUR, 30, A FARMER IN Pakistan, climbed up the side of a slurry tank to rescue one of his chickens, but lost his grip and fell in. When he failed to resurface, his three brothers and a cousin climbed up after him. All four lost their balance and fell head-first into the tank. All five men drowned. *(London) Eve. Standard, 5 Feb 2002.*

⫻ A MAN AT A FISH SAUCE FACTORY IN the Vietnamese coastal town of Phan Thiet, 118 miles (190km) northeast of Ho Chi Minh City, fell into a sauce tank on 21 October 2002. Four other workers, including the man's wife, tried to rescue him but were overcome by fumes from the fermenting fish. All five lay at the bottom of the 7.2ft (2.2m) tank for some time before being dragged out. One of the rescuers, a 34-year-old man, died after being taken to the Binh Thuan provincial hospital. *[R] 22 Oct 2002.*

⫻ SEVEN EGYPTIAN WORKERS DROWNED IN a vat of animal blood that they had been assigned to clean up at a slaughterhouse on 12 August 2003. The bodies of the men, aged between 18 and 40, were found at a farm in Qweirah, outside the Red Sea port of Aqaba in Jordan. They each drowned trying to save the other after the first worker fell in. "The blood was thick and filled with clots," said a farm manager, "making it difficult to swim." *[AP] 13 Aug 2003.*

FIVE VILLAGERS WERE SUFFOCATED IN western India on 9 August 2006 when they jumped into a dry well to save an injured pigeon. A young boy was the first to jump in, and the others followed, trying to help him. The incident took place in Jhalabordi village, about 55 miles (88km) from Ahmedabad, the chief city of Gujarat. *[R] 10 Aug 2006.*

A CLASSIC "SHIT HITS THE CLAN" TRAGEDY unfolded in Uzbekistan in August 2006. A father and son were digging a 23ft (7m) overflow pit for an existing outdoor latrine in the southern rural province of Surkhondaryo when the sides collapsed engulfing the two men in sewage. Five neighbours then rushed to their aid, lowering themselves into the pit, but died from inhaling poisonous gas. *[AP] 14 Aug 2006.*

EIGHT MEMBERS OF A FAMILY – THREE adults and five children – plus a teenage friend drowned in northern India after jumping into a 10ft (3m) -deep pond to rescue each other when two boys plunged in to retrieve their football. "Apparently, each one's bid to save the other led them to cling to each other, with the result that all of them drowned," said a police spokesman in Allahabad. *Gold Coast (Queensland) Bulletin, 12 April 2007.*

SCOTT SHOWALTER, 33, A DAIRY FARMER in Harrisonburg, Virginia, tried to transfer manure from a small pit to a larger one on 2 July 2007. A pipe became clogged and he climbed into the pit to fix the blockage, but he was overcome by methane. Farm worker Amous Stoltzfus, 24, climbed into the pit in an attempt to rescue the farmer. When the men failed to re-emerge, Mr Showalter's wife Phyllis, 34, and then her daughters Shayla, 11, and Christina, nine, made they way in. The bodies of all five were later recovered. *[AP] Sun, 4 July 2007.*

A COUPLE AND THEIR GRANDDAUGHTER were found dead in the basement of their house in Dnepropetrovsk, Ukraine, on 19 June 2010. It transpired that in an effort to exterminate rats in the basement, the grandfather, 71, had attached a hosepipe to his car's exhaust, put the other end through the basement window, and started the engine. After retiring upstairs for some time, he went to see whether any rats had died, but the concentration of carbon monoxide caused him to pass out. When he failed to return, his wife, 77, investigated and also fainted. The same later happened with their 29-year-old granddaughter. The three bodies were found when a second granddaughter went to investigate. Authorities said she was herself lucky to survive. *Pravda, via D.Record, 22 June, and D.Telegraph, 29 Jun 2010.*

OVER SIX DAYS IN NOVEMBER 2002, IN A string of apparently unconnected incidents, six men jumped into the fast-flowing River Slaney in County Wexford, Ireland. At 9am on Monday, 11 November, Peter Barron, 41, jumped into the river off a bridge in Enniscorthy after delivering his two children to school. His body was still missing a week later. At 1.35am on Saturday, 15 November, David Kehoe, 28, was seen jumping into the river from the bridge. His body was recovered later that morning.

Four men jumped into the river on Sunday, 17 November, three of whom drowned. At 1.35am, Billy Dwyer, 34, was seen jumping from the same bridge. His body was not immediately recovered. At 4am, a man believed to be from Latvia, 39 or "in his late twenties", jumped from the bridge and was rescued. At 11pm, John Foley, 19, jumped in at Bunclody about 13 miles (21km) away, and his body was recovered three hours later. Finally, some time before midnight, a man aged 23 jumped from a bridge in Wexford.

There had been 24 deaths in the Enniscorthy-to-Wexford stretch of the river over 27 years; then there were five in a week. "Nobody knows what to make of it," said Sgt Mick Morrisey, the Garda sergeant in Enniscorthy. "The last [death in the river] we had was three years ago next February. There is a dark cloud over Enniscorthy at the moment." *Irish Times, 19+20 Nov; Scotland on Sunday, 1 Dec 2002.*

D JAGGAIAH, A FARMER IN RATTA KANNA village 730km (454 miles) from Hyderabad in the southern Indian state of Andhra Pradesh, died on 18 March 2006 after drinking moonshine believed to have been brought in from neighbouring Orissa. Ten villagers attending his cremation died after toasting him with smuggled brew, while a further 16 were in critical condition in hospital. Officials in Orissa were also investigating whether the deaths were linked to those of 13 people in villages near the border between the two states who had died in the subsequent two days, reportedly after consuming homemade liquor. The drink, which sold for about 8p a bottle, was made from industrial spirit, with added vegetables, battery acid and pieces of old rubber tyres, boiled and distilled. Cheers! *[R] 21 Mar 2006.*

⟋⫽ AUSTRIAN TRAIN DRIVER HANS FICHLER, 45, was given a few hours to recover after his Eurocity train ran over an 18-year-old boy on the way to Brebenz. He switched trains to make the return journey, and then ran over and killed two policemen and a coroner who were collecting the youngster's body from the track. Mr Fichler, who was cleared of any blame, was treated for shock. *ASLEF (Associated Society of Locomotive Engineers and Firemen) Journal, Feb 2007.*

CHAPTER 19

They Died on the Job

The world of work offers rich pickings for the Grim
Reaper - especially when wood chippers or large
amounts of liquefied chocolate are involved...

ALAN WARDOUR, 52, DIED ON 23 AUGUST 1998 after falling 30ft (9m) into a vat of molten zinc at the South East Galvanising Company in Witham, Essex. Workmates saw him fall from an overhead crane gantry into the 500°C (932°F) metal, used for galvanising window frames and doors. Despite completely disappearing beneath the surface, he managed to climb out unaided and was rushed to hospital in Chelmsford, where he died later with 100 per cent burns. *(London) Eve. Standard, Halifax Eve. Courier, 24 Aug 1998.*

YONI CORDON, 19, DIED AFTER FALLING into a 1,200-gallon vat of liquefied milk chocolate on 23 July 2002. He was found by fellow workers at the sweet factory run by the Kargher Corporation in Hatfield, Pennsylvania. Police believe he had been working on a platform near the opening of the 7ft (2m) deep vat, which was used for mixing and melting chocolate. Nobody saw him fall and it was not known how long he had been submerged. "It was just like quicksand," said the aptly-named Jim Viscusi, the assistant chief of the Volunteer Medical Service Corps of nearby Lansdale, which was the first rescue unit on the scene. Another death-by-chocolate in Pennsylvania took place in 1974, when a certain Robert CH Hershey fell into a vat at the Pepperidge Farm processing plant in a Downington. *New York Times, early 1974; [AP] Philadelphia Daily News, 25 July 2002.*

VINCENT SMITH II, A CASUAL WORKER AT a Cocoa Services Inc. processing plant in Camden, New Jersey, died on 8 July 2009 after he fell into an 8ft (2.4m) tank that was mixing and melting chocolate to be used in Hershey's candy. The 29-year-old was standing on a platform and tossing blocks of solid, raw chocolate into the tank, which was heated to nearly 50°C (120°F). One of his co-workers on the platform rushed to turn the machine off and the other two tried to pull him out, but he had been struck by a mixing paddle and was dead when firefighters pulled out his chocolate-coated body. *Philadelphia Inquirer, 8 July 2009.*

RESCUERS FOUND THE FROZEN BODY OF Virglio Mernadino, 57, buried under a mountain of frozen food that had fallen from five 50ft (15m)-high racks at the Versacold warehouse in Brampton, Ontario, on 23 August 2003. He had been working alone, stacking pallets. Five of the racks holding thousands of 16cwt (800kg)-pallets were found toppled over. *[AP] 28 Aug 2003.*

A FACTORY WORKER WAS SCALDED TO DEATH when half a ton of spinach soup exploded over him in December 2002. Zacharia Conteh, 34, had the job of opening a giant pressure cooker and adding the milk and cream at the New Covent Garden Soup Company factory in Harlesden, west London. A safety device should have prevented him from doing so until the mixture had cooled. The father of two, from Deptford, died a month later in hospital. *Sun, D.Express, 5 Dec 2002.*

A SERBIAN WINE GROWER DROWNED IN cabernet sauvignon in February 2007. Miloslav Simonovic, 38, was changing a light bulb in his wine cellar in the town of Negotin when he fell off the ladder. He was knocked unconscious and found by police head first in the barrel, with his feet sticking out. *(London) Eve. Standard, 23 Feb 2007.*

A JAPANESE PAPER-RECYCLING COMPANY found the body of one its workers in a block of compressed paper in March 2009. A police spokesman said: "Officers rushed to the site and saw a man's head and arms showing on the side of the paper block… we first feared that the body was dismembered, but actually it was folded and crushed." The man was a 69-year-old part-time worker at the recycling plant in central Aichi prefecture. He was identified by a key found on him. Police were unsure whether the case was a murder or an accident. *Canberra Times, 3 Mar 2009.*

ROBERT AHRENS, 36, DIED ON 30 MAY 2005 when he fell into a meat grinder at an abattoir in Narrogin, 120 miles (192km) southeast of Perth in Western Australia. The machine had to be taken apart to allow the body to be recovered. Brian Morse, 54, the owner of a tree-trimming service in Loveland, Colorado, was killed in a similar way on 28 December when he was pulled into a wood chipper by his gloved hand. *(Sydney) D.Telegraph, 1 June; Shreveport (LA) Times, 30 Dec 2005.*

MIGUEL VARGAS, 44, WAS BEHEADED when a rope around his neck was dragged into a wood chipper. He was part of a five-man crew trimming trees on a suburban street in Tampa, Florida. A rope used by one of his colleagues somehow slipped over his neck while he was feeding branches into the chipper. He desperately fought to avoid being pulled into the machine, but couldn't reach the emergency shut-off button. The noose tightened around his neck and pulled his head from his body. *telegraph.co.uk, 27 Sept; Sun, 28 Sept 2010.*

CHAPTER 20

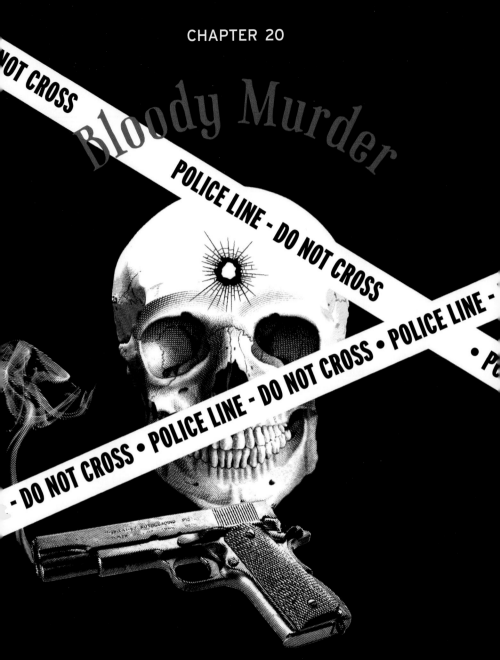

Bloody Murder

Old-fashioned homicide is all too common,
sad to say, but some murders are so bizarre
that they deserve special mention...

A WOMAN, TIRED OF CONSTANT bickering with her mother-in-law, killed her and fed her to the rest of the family. Zeng Yangxiong, 23, from Heping village in China's south-western Sichuan province, killed Wan Weichen with a metal bar after a row. As the family searched for Wan after her disappearance on 4 May 1999, Zeng was feeding them the stewed remains. Zeng confessed to the killing after uneaten body parts were found in a field. *[AFP] 23 June 1999.*

ELIZABETH RENÉE OTTE, 19, from Lanexa, Virginia, killed her month-old son, Joseph Lewis Martinez, on 23 September 1999 by cooking him in a microwave oven. She was jailed for five years on 14 December 2000 by a court in New Kent, Virginia. Otte, an epileptic, had seizures that were often followed by blackouts that could last for up to 50 minutes. "I can honestly say that I can't remember doing this, if I did," she said. She had stopped medication while pregnant and had suffered more than 509 seizures before and since the birth. The baby was found crammed inside the 18in (46cm) wide microwave in the home Otte shared with the baby's father, Joseph Anthony Martinez. He probably died after 10 minutes in the oven, when his blood reached 106°F (41° C).

Even though infant death-by-microwave was then unprecedented, by staggering coincidence another epileptic mother did exactly the same thing in the Netherlands a year later – on 8 September 2000. Annet Tol, 30, was about to warm a feeding bottle for her daughter Lynn when she suffered an epileptic fit. In a state of somnolence, she put the six-week-old child in the microwave oven instead of the milk. According to one report, she came round when the microwave bell rang. Another said the baby was in the oven for as long as 25 minutes. Mrs Tol retrieved Lynn from the microwave and tried frantically to revive her with cold water, but it was too late. The baby's father, Gerrie, 28, was at work at the time, leaving his wife alone in the flat in the fishing village of Volendam.

Wilmington (DE) News Journal, 28 Sept 1999; Dublin Eve. Herald, 7 Mar; De Telegraaf (Amsterdam), 9 Sept; D.Mail, 12 Sept; [AP] 26 Sept; Guardian, 15 Dec 2000.

A MOTHER WHO KILLED HER MONTH-OLD baby daughter by cooking her in a microwave oven was jailed for life without parole in Dayton, Ohio, in September 2008. China Arnold, 28, put her daughter, Paris Talley, in the microwave in 2005 after she and her boyfriend argued about whether he was the biological father. In this case there was no mention of epilepsy as a mitigating factor. *Independent, 9 Sept 2008.*

KATHERINE MARY KNIGHT, 45, WAS jailed for life without parole for murdering her common law husband John Price, 44, after he asked her to move out of his house in Aberdeen, New South Wales. Knight, an abattoir worker, stabbed him 37 times on Leap Day 2000. She then decapitated and skinned his body, hung the complete pelt from a meat hook in the living room, put his head in a cooking pot, and baked flesh sliced from his buttocks. The human steaks were then arranged on plates with gravy and cooked vegetables and left as meals for the son and daughter of the deceased accompanied by vindictive notes. *[AFP] Yorkshire Post, 9 Nov 2001.*

IN THE EARLY HOURS OF 5 FEBRUARY, Roland Z, 42, bludgeoned his 76-year-old mother to death, flayed her, and wore her skin around the streets of the Dutch town of Vlaardingen, shouting Biblical quotations. It was the night of a carnival, so passers-by thought he was wearing a very convincing carnival costume. After about 90 minutes he started directing traffic at a busy crossroads, and motorists called the police. Roland Z immediately confessed to the murder of his mother, saying that he was performing God's will. He had draped himself in her skin (weighing 33lb/15kg) and made his nocturnal parade to humiliate himself before God. Rather superfluously, a doctor pronounced that he was suffering from "religious madness". He was detained for psychiatric assessment. *[AP] 19 Feb; Sunday Mercury, 20 Feb; The Hague Times (Netherlands), 25 Feb 2005.*

A MAN WAS ON TRIAL IN NORWAY IN February 2010 for shooting dead his mother and cutting her body into "bite-sized" cubes with a chainsaw – because she refused to read a book he liked. The 40-year-old recommended *Girl in the Cellar* by Austrian kidnap victim Natascha Kampusch, but his mother didn't fancy it. *Sun, 16 Feb 2010.*

CAGE FIGHTER JARROD WYATT, 26, RIPPED out the heart of his training partner, Taylor Powell, 21, while he was still alive. He also cut out his tongue and tore off most of his face. The gory attack took place in Klamath, California, in March 2010. Police found Wyatt standing naked over his dead friend surrounded by body parts. He said he had drunk a cup of tea made from hallucinogenic mushrooms and became convinced Powell was possessed by the Devil. He was charged with first-degree murder, aggravated mayhem and torture. Powell's cause of death was recorded as blood loss due to having his heart removed while still alive. *Sun, 31 May; Metro, 3 June 2010.*

CHAPTER 21

Gone, but Forgotten

It's sad to think that no one even notices
when some of us pass on - or at best mistake the
corpse for a piece of modern art...

WOLFGANG DIRCKS SAT IN FRONT OF HIS television set for five years, the lights on his Christmas tree flashing beside him, and none of his Hamburg neighbours noticed that he was dead. "Someone said once that he had gone off to a home," said a neighbour. He was eventually discovered as a skeleton with a TV listings magazine open on his lap at 5 December 1993 and a half-finished bottle of beer beside him. He would have been 43 years old at that time. The television had blown a fuse, but the Christmas tree lights were still flickering.

Mr Dircks, a former toolsmith, was divorced and crippled after a hip operation, and he apparently discouraged people from getting to know him by threatening to whip them. According to the *Bild* newspaper, an unknown person emptied his letterbox periodically, which might otherwise have been a clue, and his two immediate neighbours in the 18-flat block had moved in only four years earlier, so they had never seen him. Bills were paid by direct debit from the account of his mother, who still lived in an old people's home. Only when the account ran dry did his landlord come to see what had happened. *[R] D.Mail, 19 Nov; Independent, Times, D.Telegraph, 20 Nov 1998.*

INVESTIGATING A REPORT OF BURST PIPES on 15 February 2007, police in Southampton, Long Island, found the mummified body of Vincenzo Riccardi, 70, sitting in a chair in front of his television, which was still on (channel unspecified). He had died more than a year earlier, apparently of natural causes. He had not been heard from since December 2005. Neighbours said he had diabetes and had gone blind in his 50s. (How then, we might ask, could he have been watching television?) His house was up a long driveway and could not be seen from the street. The lack of humidity had preserved his features. *Los Angeles Times, 18 Feb 2007.*

ANOTHER PERSON WHO SAT DEAD IN FRONT of a blaring television was Carol Vincent, 40, whose body was found in her tiny studio flat in Wood Green, north London, in January 2006, when a housing officer broke in after rent arrears had run into thousands of pounds. There was a bag of shopping by her side and Christmas presents she had wrapped but never delivered. She had lost contact with her siblings and had been dead for more than two years. Post dating back to November 2003 was piled up behind the door. The heating had been on all the time, and her body was so badly decomposed she had to be formally identified by comparing her teeth with dental records and a photograph of her smiling. Cause of death could not be established. *Guardian, D.Telegraph, D.Mail, 14 April 2006.*

WORKMEN INVESTIGATING A WATER LEAK at a high-rise apartment block in Newcastle upon Tyne in August 2006 found the skeleton of Robert Frame, a 57-year-old former sailor, sitting in an armchair facing a television. (We are not told whether it was on or not). The body was next to a ready meal with a best-before date of late December 2004. His benefits had been paid into his bank and his council rent taken by direct debit. In July 2007, the coroner recorded an open verdict. *D.Mail, 14 July 2007.*

THE CORPSE OF A 59-YEAR-OLD MAN WAS FOUND in his bed in the German city of Essen on 10 May 2007. Police said he had probably died of natural causes on 30 November 2000, the date he received a letter from the Welfare Office found in the apartment. Next to the bed were an open television guide and Deutschemark coins, which went out of circulation after the Euro was introduced in 2002. "No one missed him," police said. *D.Telegraph, 11 May; Irish Examiner, 12 May 2007.*

A FINNISH TAX OFFICIAL DROPPED DEAD at his desk in 2004 and nobody noticed for two days. The tabloid *Ilta-Sanomat* reported that none of the 30 people who were in the same department as the unnamed 60-year-old auditor realised that he was not just silently poring over papers in the Helsinki office. Anita Wickstroem, the director, told AFP news agency: "He was working alone and his friends and colleagues who used to have lunch or coffee with him were busy." The story of George Turklebaum, a New York proof reader whose death in an open plan office went unnoticed for five days in October 2000, turned out to be an urban legend; however, maybe this time it really happened.

In March 2008, office workers in Romania also took two days to notice that one of their colleagues had died at her desk. Despite their open-plan office, civil servants in the accounting department of an office in Botosani didn't think anything was wrong with Aurica Vladimirescu, 49. "She sometimes had a few drinks at midday," said a spokesman. "We thought she was just taking a rest." As our only source for this story was the free London paper *Metro*, maybe this is apocryphal. *BBC News, 19 Jan; [AFP] 20 Jan 2004. Metro, 19 Mar 2008.*

THE BODY OF A CZECH MAN WHO DIED IN THE bath lay unnoticed for 12 years – even though neighbours complained about flies in the building every summer. Frantisek Konvicka, 62 when he died, was found in May 2007 when bailiffs turned up to evict him from his flat in the town of Novy Jicin for not paying his council taxes. "We never suspected anything," said neighbour Rudolf Jurica. "We assumed he was just a very private man." *Metro, 24 May 2007.*

JUSTIN AND COLLEEN MCKEEN, HOUSEHUNT-ING in Wisconsin in May 2007, walked into the bedroom of a house they were inspecting in Janesville and found the body of the homeowner, 55-year-old Linda O'Leary, who was later assessed to have died two weeks earlier. Linda Chabucos-Galow, the estate agent, had set up the visit without knowing the homeowner's identity. She was in the living room when she heard the couple scream. Police said there was no indication of foul play. *Guardian, 3 May 2007.*

JORDI GIRO BOUGHT A FLAT IN THE COSTA Brava resort of Rosas in Catalonia at an auction after the previous owner defaulted on her payments. When he entered the flat for the first time on 12 May 2007, he found her mummified body sitting on the sofa. Maria Luisa Zamora had failed to keep up payments on her mortgage because she had in fact died of natural causes in 2001. Neither her estranged husband nor her children in Madrid registered a missing persons report for the 55-year-old. Police believed the salty sea air had preserved the body. *BBC News, 16 May 2007.*

A CAR CARRYING THE BODY OF NELSON Contreras was hit by a truck in the Chilean town of Eistein, leaving the coffin and flowers in the street. No one helped the Contreras family pick up the coffin or gather the scattered flowers, because both police and passers-by thought it was an art installation in homage to the surreal painter Roberto Matta Echaurren, who had died that day. Osvaldo Brandt, nephew of Mr Contreras, told *La Cuarta* newspaper: "After almost an hour we managed to get a cab, put the coffin inside and continue on our way to the cemetery." *Ananova, 25 Nov 2002.*

ON 14 NOVEMBER 2003, HUNGARIAN POLICE removed the corpse of a man believed to have hanged himself at least a year earlier. Builders and students at Budapest's University of Arts had initially mistaken the body it for a modern sculpture; it had hung for a whole day in a garden building before onlookers realised what it was. The building, in campus grounds crowded with different types of sculpture, had been closed five years earlier pending reconstruction work. "The biggest mystery is why the body had mummified," said police spokesman Laszlo Bartha. "The skin had shrivelled and turned to leather, which is why nobody realised it was a corpse, not a sculpture." At the time of the report, the man had not been identified. *[R,AFP] 17 Nov 2003.*

PASSERS-BY IGNORED A DEAD MAN decked out in sadomasochistic gear and hanging by a spiked dog collar from a fence – thinking it was an ad for a sex shop. Manhattan police were finally alerted by a dog walker and were trying to identify the man. Foul play was not suspected. *News of the World, 1 Oct 2006.*

A BODY SLUMPED OVER A CHAIR ON THE balcony of a third-floor apartment in Los Angeles drew stares for three days, but no calls to the police. Neighbours noticed the body on 12 October, but thought it was part of a Hallowe'en display. When someone eventually investigated, they found it was a real dead man. Mostafa Mahmoud Zayed, 75, had apparently committed suicide; he had a single gunshot wound to the eye. *New York Daily News, 18 Oct 2009.*

FORTEAN TIMES WOULD LIKE TO THANK:
The many readers who, over the years, have sent in the newspaper clippings or
Internet links from which the stories in this volume have been compiled.

GET INVOLVED – BECOME A **FORTEAN TIMES** CLIPSTER!
Regular clipsters have provided the lifeblood of **Fortean Times** since it began
in 1973. One of the delights for the editors is receiving packets of clips from
Borneo or Brazil, Saudi Arabia or Siberia. We invite you to join in the fun and send
in anything weird, from trade journals, local newspapers, extracts from obscure
tomes, or library newspaper archives.
To minimise the time spent on preparing clippings for a Fort Sort, we ask
that you cut them out and not fold them too small. Mark each clip (on the front,
where possible) with the source, date and your name, so that we can credit you
in the listing when we use the material. For UK local and overseas clips, please
give the town of publication. For foreign language clips, we appreciate brief
translations. To avoid confusion over day and month, please write the date in this
form: 10 May 2011. If you send photocopies, copy on one side of the paper only.

Mail to: **Fortean Times, PO Box 2409, London NW5 4NP, UK**
E-mail: **sieveking@forteantimes.com**
or post on the FT website at **www.forteantimes.co.uk,**
where there is a contributor's guide.

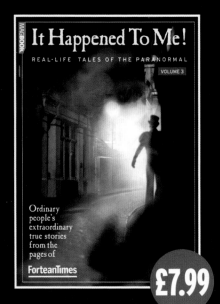

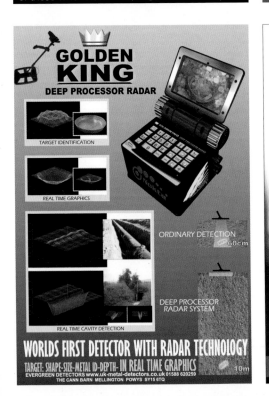